100 PERCENT **MORTALITY**

100 PERCENT MORTALITY

15 Stories of Excuses, Mistakes, and Misunderstandings in Estate Planning

BY

DEBRA KOVEN

Published by Best Seller Publishing®, St. Augustine, FL
Best Seller Publishing® is a registered trademark.
Printed in the United States of America.
ISBN: 978-1-962595-46-9

This publication is designed to provide accurate and authoritative information with regard to the subject matter covered. It is sold with the understanding that the publisher is not engaged in rendering legal, accounting, or other professional advice. If legal advice or other expert assistance is required, the services of a competent professional should be sought. The opinions expressed by the author in this book are not endorsed by Best Seller Publishing® and are the sole responsibility of the author rendering the opinion.

Disclaimer: Debra Koven is licensed to practice exclusively in California. The information shared in her book is general and intended to educate, clarify, and motivate—it is not intended to serve as legal advice, nor should it substitute for the counsel of an attorney authorized to practice in your jurisdiction.

To illustrate the information shared, the author has provided client-based stories in which personal details have been changed in the interest of preserving privacy and attorney-client privilege.

For more information, please write:
Best Seller Publishing®
1775 US-1 #1070
St. Augustine, FL 32084
or call 1 (626) 765-9750
Visit us online at: www.BestSellerPublishing.org

Dedication

For my beautiful daughter, Nyssa—
the inspiration for everything.

Contents

Acknowledgements

Writing a book is a journey that stretches far beyond the author's solitary efforts. Although for me the writing portion was not exactly a collaborative endeavor, I found that I garnered support, guidance, and encouragement from numerous individuals who played indispensable roles in its creation. In this humble space, I extend my deepest gratitude to those whose unwavering support has made this book a reality.

TO MY MENTORS

First, to my original legal mentor, William Koontz, who authored the foreword—your wisdom and experience shaped my thinking and guided me early on in my legal career. You always took me on an intellectual journey, navigating the ins and outs of litigation and allowing me the freedom to grow and develop my own personal style. Your insights, critiques, and guidance were invaluable in refining my skills as a litigator and counselor at law. I am profoundly grateful for the privilege of learning from your expertise. Over the years that we worked together, your friendship and support were a vital component of my personal and professional success. I have always looked up to you and still sit in awe of your deep and heartfelt love of the law. Plus, you are a diehard Bruins fan!

To Ali Katz—the creator and founder of New Law Business Model—and my one true estate planning mentor. Where to even begin? Your vision of what a law practice should be, your ability to convey the most effective way to represent our clients, and your love for and dedication to the art of estate planning all makes me so proud to be a Personal Family Lawyer! Your approach has taught me that I can provide excellent service to clients, be an entrepreneur in a law practice that I love, and still find work-life balance that sustains me into the future. You truly inspired me to view the business of lawyering in a whole different way that changed the course of my career. I am eternally grateful. To my original NLBM coach, Allison Osborne, and to the family of PFLs across this country—your support, mentorship, friendship, and encouragement have been a significant driving force.

TO MY FAMILY

To my family—specifically, my husband, Brad, my sister Brenda, my niece Brooke, and my nephew Josh—your love, patience, and belief in me provided the foundation upon which I built this work. Thank you for being my steadfast pillars. To my incredible daughter, Nyssa—I love you more than words could ever express, and I only want to be the best possible mom I can be for you! It is my hope that you will always know that you are my number one priority, my reason for getting up every day.

TO MY PUBLISHER AND EDITORIAL TEAM

To the dedicated professionals at BSP, whose commitment to excellence transformed my little stories into a polished book. Rob

Kosberg, Bob Harpole, and the rest of the BSP Team—you have all played a crucial role in bringing this book to the world. Thank you for your expertise and passion. And to my creative book coach, Matt Schnarr, who never seemed to tire of my endless questions and concerns over the content of this book, who seemed to not only get my bizarre sense of humor but also truly understood my goals and vision for this book. Your help and guidance are deeply appreciated!

TO MY FRIENDS AND COLLEAGUES

To my beloved friends and colleagues who offered valuable and unwavering encouragement throughout this process. Your belief in me has been a constant source of motivation. To the members of Local Anchor, South Bay Mommies and Daddies—this online community is where so many of my clients have found me. It is an honor and a privilege to serve the families from this group—all of whom share the goal of ensuring their kids are always well protected in whatever circumstances may arise.

TO MY READERS

To you, dear readers, who hold this book in your hands or read it on your screens, your interest in my work is the ultimate reward for my labor. I hope this book enriches your life in some way, and I am deeply grateful for your time and attention.

With heartfelt thanks,
Debra

Foreword

by William Koontz

I've known Debra Koven for nearly 35 years now. My first encounter with her is rather vague to me, as she was a paralegal at a local defense firm. I don't think I knew that she was studying law. As I got to know her better, I appreciated what an exceptionally hard worker she was, yet one who always found time to help where help was needed.

One of the lawyers at her firm left to start his own practice, rented an office from me, and then brought Debra with him. By that time, she was a lawyer. Debra, always courageous and assertive, began to display those attributes in pursuit of justice for her clients. The cases then were personal injury matters; I don't mind admitting that I was astonished by her fortitude, zest for the law, and self-assurance in dealing with older male lawyers with far more experience. She was undaunted when going to trial, and her attitude was markedly to never surrender—even when she would tell me during her trial of significant unforeseen setbacks.

She was ever optimistic of the outcome.

After having left to practice elsewhere, I was fortunate enough to convince Debra to join me in the same suite she had previously worked in. We became close friends and colleagues. I found her to be not just passionate in her pursuit of what she believed was right but compassionate as well. She was the only lawyer of many who were solicited to go to the county hospital to interview a homeless man with a dubious case—a case she and I worked to a dramatic result for the client. A client who felt so indebted to her that he treated her as a member of his family.

Around that time, Debra phoned me and said she had gotten a call from a family in central California regarding a serious accident resulting in the death of one family member and significant injury to others. We flew to central California in the rain to meet with them. Debra took the lead in speaking to the matriarch—her even tone, concise explanation, and forthright approach was exceptional. A talent of hers, I would learn over the next few years, was not just limited to speaking skills but writing as well. I was in court before the court of appeals when several justices from the bench praised her concise and excellent writing skills.

I have less contact with her now but speak to her frequently. I follow her online and see photos of her and her daughter, her husband, and the direction her career has taken. She has abandoned the frenzied world of personal injury, and I think this has served her perfectly. She has found a wonderful balance between work and family, work that uses all her talent as a lawyer and a human being.

Introduction

I consider myself exceptionally blessed in regard to becoming a lawyer. I knew from an early age—ten, to be exact—that I wanted to be a lawyer. How did I know this? No clue. I did not know a single attorney at that point. No member of my family was a lawyer. In the 1970s, there were no shows on television depicting lawyers. *Perry Mason* had long since ended, and *LA Law* didn't start up until the mid-1980s—damn, I'm aging myself. So, I truly have no idea how I decided I would be a lawyer, other than knowing that I wanted to help people in some way. I always say that I did not call the law, the law called me.

My parents were very much against the idea and discouraged me. I suppose that is one reason I was so adamant in pursuing it and proving them wrong. (That statement alone might give you some insight as to who I am!) I was on a very distinct path, and while it was not an easy road by any means, I was persistent and basically reinvented the wheel as I progressed through, since I had no one to show me the ropes. It is most assuredly not the path most people need to take today.

This was more than 30 years ago. When I initially passed the California bar examination, I was not aware of many women lawyers—other than those teaching in law school or taking subordinate roles in law firms where I'd worked along the way. Back in those days, most of the women working in the law were court reporters, secretaries, or office managers. I don't need to recount all of the horror stories of sexual harassment, gender discrimination, and overall poor treatment I encountered during my early years as a civil litigator. But much of that shaped the type of lawyer I knew I did NOT want to be and led me to breaking away from the firm mentality and going off on my own.

My Way

For the first 20-plus years of my career, I was a trial lawyer. Yep, I was that gal in the suit, carrying a briefcase and dragging a roller with two or three file boxes loaded onto it. I tried many, many cases during those years and was fortunately pretty good at it. I could think on my feet and argue with the best of them. And I had no qualms about speaking in front of 12 strangers—after spending early morning hours puking my nerves away in the courthouse bathroom—who were impaneled to determine whether my client proved their case and would receive a financial award. I won more cases than I lost. I had a couple of truly amazing mentors to help me along the way. I believe I developed a good reputation in the community.

The cases came in, and I got to pick and choose the ones I wanted to take on. Generally, the tougher the case, the more likely I was to accept it. I liked taking those previously disenfranchised plaintiffs, turned down by other lawyers and who really needed the help . . .

- The homeless guy who got hit by a garbage truck in an alley

- The model who was portrayed as having a communicable disease in a medication ad that was personalized without their consent
- The woman who was beat up in a fast-food parking lot even as she begged the employees to call 911

You get the picture.

I built a nice practice and worked hard. Some weeks it was 70 hours or more. I rarely took vacations. The work was rewarding but exhausting. Again, I got into the law to help people, to be of service. As such, I was not one to take time away for myself.

Everything changed in 2010. My daughter was born. I knew I needed to get out of the courtroom. I wanted to be a mom. I knew that was the most important job I would ever have. But I still had bills to pay and needed to work.

The idea of doing estate planning had been in the back of my mind for a year or more before my daughter was born. But I'll be honest, I was super passionate about trial work. It not only kept my adrenaline going, but it also kept me mentally stimulated. Each case had its own set of unique issues to deal with. I was very invested in the cases I took and in the success of my clients. I did not see how estate planning could ever equal what I personally got from being a civil litigator.

Nevertheless, the desire to be at home with my daughter far outweighed the personal gratification of continuing to be a trial attorney. And boy, am I glad that it did.

When I first started doing estate planning, I knew very little about how to go about it, other than what I had learned back in law school many years prior. I had done some probate work during my litigation years, and I had written a few Wills and Trusts for clients along the way. But I needed to dig deep into continuing education classes to bring me up to speed on how to go about helping clients in this new practice area. So, that is exactly what I did. I also developed relationships with some incredible mentors who helped steer me in the right direction. To this day, I still seek their counsel on issues that arise where I need a second opinion.

During the course of expanding my expertise in this area of practice, I found that the traditional estate planning attorneys were basically just document-producing firms that created a set of documents for their clients. Providing actual service to those clients did not seem to be part of the agenda. I knew that if this was an area of practice I was going to engage in, it was not going to happen the "traditional" way.

So, What Is an Estate Plan?

Basically, an estate plan serves as a set of instructions regarding how you want your assets to be passed down, to whom you want them to pass, and when you want them to pass to those beneficiaries. By creating a plan, you also send a message to your loved ones that you care enough to put your affairs in order in hopes of protecting them—keeping them out of court and out of conflict by establishing exactly what you want to happen.

A basic estate plan consists of several documents that provide these instructions both during your life (in the event of incapacity) and when you pass away. The documents I'm referring to are as follows:

1. A Revocable Living Trust
2. A Will
3. A Power of Attorney (to deal with financial matters during incapacity)
4. A Healthcare Power of Attorney

5. A Healthcare Living Will
6. A HIPAA waiver

A comprehensive estate plan includes the above and more.

Most people have some familiarity with a Will. Generally, a Will dictates distribution of your assets upon your death. It nominates an individual as an executor or personal representative who will work with the court to pay off your creditors and potentially distribute your assets according to what your Will indicates. I say "potentially" because, you should be aware, a Will can be contested in court.

A court must authenticate the Will. So, there is a possibility that if someone contests your Will, it may not be authenticated if the contest prevails, and the Will could fail—meaning the listing of your desires is completely disregarded and your assets would pass according to the law in your state. The state's methodology of dispersing your assets may or may not be in alignment with what your Will indicated in the first place. You should also be aware that depending on the state, the probate process is completely open to the public—meaning anyone can go to the court and request to look at the files (more on that in Chapter 2).

The point here is, if you create *only a Will,* it is not guaranteed to be upheld, but it is *guaranteed* to go through a court process. Throughout the course of this book, I'll be talking about what that means and why you likely want to avoid it.

The primary way to avoid this court process is to have a Revocable Living Trust created. In essence, a Trust is an agreement by which you determine how to distribute your assets, to whom, and when those distributions are to occur. A Trust serves to maintain the privacy of your desires. There is no court process or oversight, but rather you appoint someone called a Successor Trustee to handle carrying out your stated wishes after you pass away. When you create a Trust, you transfer your assets into the Trust during your lifetime and you manage them yourself, just as you would in any other instance. But creating a Revocable Living Trust is a planning strategy, which also demonstrates to your loved ones how important it is to you to save them the court "experience" as well as saving your own estate the potentially high cost of having a judge make your decisions for you.

The other documents included in your estate plan are more about dealing with possible incapacity. A power of attorney will handle your day-to-day financial affairs, while your healthcare agent will make medical decisions or carry out those decisions that you've already made, which are put into the legal documentation. Moreover, in my office, we also do a whole set of standalone documents to protect your children in the event that you pass away before they reach the age of majority. That is part of the comprehensive estate plan. More on all of the above later in this book.

What's Your Excuse?

So far, you have to be thinking to yourself, *Gee, this is fun stuff, I truly love thinking about my incapacity and dying. NOT*. I know it's extremely maudlin, but truly, I've done the research, and I've seen the studies. We humans have a 100 percent mortality rate. We are all going to die at some point. Surprise! Not. It may sound harsh, but it's a reality.

Doesn't it make much more sense to plan this out while you're still alive and have the capacity to do so? Yep, I think so too. Nevertheless, so many people have yet to do their estate plan.

According to a survey conducted by Caring LLC in 2021, it was found that *only 32 percent* of American adults had a Will or another type of estate planning document in place. The American Association of Retired Persons (AARP) has compiled similar statistics.[1] This indicates that a significant portion of the population in the United States does not have a comprehensive estate plan in place. Moreover, it is worth noting that a survey conducted by Caring LLC in 2019 found that 57 *percent* of American adults with children under the age of 18 had not designated legal guardians for their children in the event something happens to them.

There's any number of excuses that I've seen over the course of my practice, and that is the theme of this book. What I've done is create avatars from people whom I've actually worked with, to explore the questions, concerns, and reasons behind people's aversions to taking this important and vital step to prepare for their ultimate demise.

Who am I? And why should you, the reader, listen to me describe estate planning? As I've said, I have been an attorney for more than 30 years. My practice, and my focus, is on families with minor children because I'm a mom, and I believe parenthood to be my number one job. But having the wisdom and experience of an attorney in practice for over 30 years, I come from a different perspective, and I bring both to the table.

While I love helping those families ensure that their minor kids never wind up somewhere the family would not want (child protective services, an inappropriate relative, etc.), I help all kinds of people. That is what you will find as you read through the stories in this book. The excuses for not getting a plan in place are not limited to only those with littles in the household.

The chapters ahead of you are for every adult who has a pulse but has yet to get their estate plan put together. I know. It is a rough topic. It is seemingly very scary. Whether you admit to it out loud or not—most of you know in the back of your mind that this is something you, your parents, siblings, or extended family

1 "2023 Wills and Estate Planning Study" by Rachel Lustbader, Staff Editor, Caring LLC (Online Article)

needs to do—you all need to do this very "adult" thing. I assure you that with the help of an experienced and trustworthy lawyer (like me), the process is not nearly as difficult or daunting as you've told yourself that it is.

Think about it. Do you really want to wait until you are in crisis mode to start the process? Do you want to risk losing assets and having your decision-making power taken away? Would you want a judge deciding who raises your minor children? I have seen some bad endings—and I truly do not want this to happen to you.

What is your excuse? Go ahead and start thinking about that now. As you read through the excuses given by the people written about in this book, I want you to think about where you see yourself. Are you like Clueless Cody or Procrastinator Paul? Or perhaps you relate to Meager Melanie and Adolescent Ava? I have seen quite a few DIY Davids, Cheap Charlies, and Unfunded Umas. Still, there are plenty of Overconfident Omars, Vibrant Vivians, and Supported Sheilas out there too. Although less common, I have helped Apathetic Andys, Superstitious Sallys, and Skeptical Sues. But maybe you'll see yourself in Prepared Patty, Isolated Irwin, or Avoidance Arnie.

Regardless of your reason for putting it off, take a hard look at these avatars, maybe note the one you think you most align with, and read that chapter first. Then, you can go back and see how they compare to the other characters I've written about.

It's likely that you've spent hours upon hours, and thousands and thousands of dollars, on things like after-school care, extracurricular activities, summer camps, and family vacations, all for the benefit of your children and loved ones. So, why would you want to waste your children's (or other loved ones') inheritance on a court process? Why wouldn't you spend a couple of hours and a bit of money getting your ducks in a row for THEIR benefit? Estate planning is something you do for your family and loved ones—but it gives you peace of mind that you have taken care of this on their behalf!

Are You Ready?

Back in my childhood days, I always wanted to write a book. I thought I would be writing a romance novel or maybe a murder mystery. Never did I think I would be writing a book about estate planning! I do want to try to keep this on the light side and inject a bit of humor and sarcasm, because the subjects of death and dying are scary. Most people don't even want to think about it, let alone discuss it with a lawyer.

Part of being an adult is taking care of the people who you love while still ensuring your own wishes are carried out. To that end, you'll see some of my snark and humor along the way. It is not intended to be disrespectful to any of the characters I write about, but rather to keep you engaged and help lighten the existential fears that many of us face around death and incapacity.

Through this book, it is my hope to help educate and guide you to understanding what estate planning actually is, and why doing it is preferable to the alternative (aka doing nothing and leaving a mess behind for a court to sort out). I know you can do this! So, let's dive in, shift perspective, discover lessons—and overcome all of those overused excuses as to why your estate plan is not done!

I'm ready if you are.

Debra Koven
www.debrakovenlaw.com

Before We Get Started . . .

Do Any of These Sound Familiar?

Before we get started, if you'd like, let's take some time to familiarize ourselves with the characters ahead. As you read through the following descriptions, do any of these points align with your concerns and questions? If so, feel free to jump around.

CHAPTER 1: SUPPORTED SHEILA & AVOIDANCE ARNIE (YOURS, MINE & MINE?)

Do you know that the type of family you have can affect the estate plan you have? Are you married? Blended family? Two earners? Sole bread earner? Before you even get to the place of having your estate plan created, you need to think about how you want your assets divided at your death, AND this is something to discuss with your spouse or significant other now. In this chapter, we'll talk about some of the conversations you should consider having with your significant other before you start planning for your eventual demise.

CHAPTER 2: PROCRASTINATOR PAUL (NO NEED TO PUT OFF TO TOMORROW IF YOU'RE GOING TO DIE TODAY)

Do you have a hard time making decisions? Are you confused about who you should give your assets to when you pass away? Are you putting off planning because you're not sure what to do? In this chapter, we'll explore how procrastination can really put a roadblock in the process for you. This chapter will show what can happen to your estate when you keep putting things off.

CHAPTER 3: CLUELESS CODY (LIVE UNDER A ROCK, AND THE PRESSURE MAY KILL YOU)

Have you thought about estate planning in the past? Do you wonder if it's something you actually need? If you don't know what an estate plan is or why you might need one, this is the chapter for you.

CHAPTER 4: THE STORY OF MEAGER MELANIE (SO, YOU THOUGHT YOU HAD NOTHING TO LOSE . . .)

Are you of the mindset that you don't have a lot of financial assets to even give to anyone when you die? Do you believe that a close family member will automatically be chosen to raise your minor child at your death? In this chapter, we're going to look at the three primary reasons you might need a plan, and why leaving it up to a court to decide who raises your child is not the best option.

CHAPTER 5: APATHETIC ANDY (100 PERCENT MORTALITY, WHETHER YOU CARE OR NOT)

Have you ever thought that estate planning is unnecessary because you'll be dead and don't really care what happens once you are gone? Does creating an estate plan really matter for you since you will be dead when it comes into play? This story reveals how personal life circumstances may have you thinking twice about not caring what happens to your assets after you die.

CHAPTER 6: A TALE OF TWO CLIENTS: SKEPTICAL SUE AND ISOLATED IRWIN (TO TRUST OR NOT TO TRUST . . . IS THAT REALLY THE QUESTION?)

Among other reasons, have you not gotten your estate plan in place because you are not sure who you can trust to handle the responsibilities? Perhaps you do not have close family members or even friends you believe you can rely on to deal with carrying out your decisions? The avatars in this chapter are in similar, yet different circumstances. Neither has that "go-to" person who can deal with the incapacity and post-death responsibilities. Here, I'll show you how these issues can be dealt with.

CHAPTER 7: DIY DAVID (WHO WANTS TO ASSEMBLE THEIR TRUST FROM IKEA?)

Are you the type who, at a minimum, will try to do most things on your own rather than seeking out a professional? Have you ever tried to fill out an online form to deal with a legal matter? In this chapter, we will look at why the DIY of legal documents can leave your loved ones with a big, hot mess.

CHAPTER 8: UNFUNDED UMA (YOU CAN'T CROSS YOUR T'S OR DOT YOUR I'S IF THERE ARE NO LETTERS)

Are you the kind of person who, once a project is done, never goes back and looks at it again? Did you create an estate plan 5, 10, or even 15 years ago and not review it since? Did a "traditional" estate planning attorney put some documents together for you and never bother to follow up to see if there were any changes that occurred that might require an update to your plan? As you read on through this chapter, you'll discover how my office does things differently than a traditional estate planning law office, and you'll understand why I say estate planning is not "one and done."

CHAPTER 9: PREPARED PATTY AND PRODIGAL PETE (WHAT'S YOURS IS YOURS)

Are you and your spouse yin and yang? Did you find that when it comes to you and your mate, opposites attract? Is one of you the CFO (chief financial officer) of the family and the other the COS (chief officer of spending)? Have you had conversations with your significant other about how money should be spent or saved? The avatars in this story could not be more different in their approach to money. Here, I will show you how multiple solutions exist within the estate planning arena for even these types of contrasting views.

CHAPTER 10: OVERCONFIDENT OMAR (KNOWING IT ALL DOESN'T MEAN YOU GET IT RIGHT)

Are you the person in the room who has the solution to every problem? Do you believe your way is always the right way? If so, you might want to skip this chapter! Here, we will explore how things can go awry if you rely on non-estate-planning documents to transfer your assets at the time of your death, and how your family might be left high and dry unless you plan appropriately while you are still alive.

CHAPTER 11: SUPERSTITIOUS SALLY (WILL DEATH TAKE A HOLIDAY?)

Are you apprehensive to talk about death? Do you fear it to the point where you cannot even have a conversation about dying or incapacity? For some, this is a cultural phenomenon, and for others, it might be generational. This chapter looks at how one family suffered because their matriarch refused to think about death, let alone get a plan in place to deal with the inevitable.

CHAPTER 12: CHEAP CHARLIE (A PENNY SAVED BY NOT ESTATE PLANNING IS A MILLION PENNIES GIFTED TO THE STATE)

Have you heard of those old sayings, "penny-wise and pound foolish" and "you get what you pay for"? Or are you intimately familiar with the value of items at the 99¢ Store? There are certain services that—if pursuing the cheapest available—will not provide the necessary protections you likely want for your family and loved ones. Such is the case with estate planning. Here, our avatar puts himself and his family at great risk because cost was the most important factor in his mind.

CHAPTER 13: ADOLESCENT AVA & COMPLETE CHERISE (YOU'RE NEVER TOO YOUNG FOR ESTATE PLANNING)

Do you feel that you are too young to think about the matters in this book? Have you managed to actually find great success in your endeavors, but are you now realizing there is more to money than simply making or spending it? Are you prepared for the worst-case scenario of unexpectedly leaving permanently or temporarily? Just because you're under 30 does not mean you don't need a plan.

CHAPTER 14: FANCIFUL FRANCINE (YOUR BEST INTERESTS ARE NOT AUTOMATED)

Are you expecting the government to automatically process and distribute your assets to whomever applicable? Do you share property ownership with other people? And do you have any loved ones who live out of your country? Unfortunately, when left to automation, it's most likely that your assets will take the probate route—and I hope by this chapter you understand the dangers of this.

CHAPTER 15: VIBRANT VIVIAN (YOU DON'T NEED TO LEARN THE HARD WAY)

Have you made any of your wishes known to friends and loved ones? Do you have family who you do not trust with those decisions? Would you like to incorporate trustworthy individuals into your plans? Accidents are sadly inevitable, and with the right names on the right lines, your care and representation can be concrete. A little effort today may surprise you in the future.

Do You Know What a Fiduciary Is?

Throughout the course of this book, I will be using the term "fiduciary" in several different scenarios. In the context of estate planning, a fiduciary refers to an individual (meaning an actual human person) or entity (such as a bank or an investment management company such as Schwab, Fidelity, or a licensed professional fiduciary) that has been entrusted with the responsibility of managing and making decisions related to the assets, finances, and well-being of another person, who has chosen or designated the fiduciary.

The individual or entity fiduciary is legally and ethically bound to act in the best interests of the beneficiary or the assets, putting the instructions, needs, and wishes of the designating party ahead of their own. Fiduciaries are held to a very high standard of care, loyalty, and honesty. They are required to act diligently, prudently, and in accordance with the wishes of the person who nominated or designated them to act as fiduciary. Breach of fiduciary duty is taken seriously and can result in legal consequences, including potential financial liability. It is important to choose fiduciaries carefully and provide clear instructions to ensure that your assets and loved ones are managed according to your intentions.

Examples of the different roles in which a person or entity might be designated as a fiduciary include the following:

> **Trustee:** A Trustee is responsible for managing and distributing assets held in a Trust according to the terms specified in the Trust document.
>
> **Executor** or **Personal Representative:** This individual is appointed in a Will to oversee the distribution of assets of an estate after the death of the testator (the person who created the Will).
>
> **Guardian:** In cases involving minor children, a guardian may be appointed to make decisions

about the children's upbringing, education, and well-being if the parents pass away.

Attorney-in-Fact or **Power of Attorney:** This individual has the authority to make financial and legal decisions on behalf of the principal (the person who granted the power of attorney).

Healthcare Proxy or **Agent:** Similar to an attorney-in-fact but focused on medical decisions, a healthcare proxy is appointed to make medical choices on behalf of the principal if they become unable to make those decisions themselves.

Okay, here we go ...

Chapter 1

Supported Sheila & Avoidance Arnie (Yours, Mine & Mine?)

Do you know that the type of family you have can affect the estate plan you have? Are you married? Blended family? Two earners? Sole bread earner? Before you even get to the place of having your estate plan created, you need to think about how you want your assets divided at your death, AND this is something to discuss with your spouse or significant other now. In this chapter, we'll talk about some of the conversations you should consider having with your significant other before you start planning for your eventual demise.

You may think there is an ego component to the work I do, because you know most lawyers love to hear themselves talk(!), but lawyers are really more than just "attorneys." We are counselors in many regards. As an estate planning attorney, I feel it is my obligation to help clients have hard conversations. Sometimes that means with family members such as siblings or parents, and sometimes between a couple themselves. Those conversations can center on illness, death, parenting styles (occasionally), how to choose guardians or successors, and a whole host of other topics. Quite frequently, those hard conversations revolve around money.

Money is far and away one of the trickier topics to talk about. I strongly believe that most people have their own unique relationship with money. Some people have a really good relationship with money, understand how it works, do not stress out about it, are able to consistently earn it, and clearly know how to manage it. Others have a more difficult and complicated relationship with money, usually because of the way they were raised. I will admit to you that I was one of the latter.

When I was growing up in my household, my parents didn't talk about money except to tell me that we didn't have enough. The conversation was limited to letting me know that we couldn't get those new jeans or take that desired vacation because we didn't have the money to do so. We were taught to save and to not indulge in frivolous spending of any kind.

I got a job at age 15 so that I could earn my own spending money. I would ride my bike to the local ice cream shop, where I worked for minimum wage, which at the time was about $3.25 an hour. I saved most of it in the interest of purchasing some things I wanted as a teenager that my parents would not buy for me.

My parents couldn't afford to send me to college. I had to learn how to apply for and manage student loans to attend UCLA—GO BRUINS!—for my undergraduate degree. I held a part-time job to help cover additional expenses, including books and supplies. I wound up working full-time at a law firm during law school, struggling to support myself and still get through the rigorous class schedule. There were days when I needed to choose between paying rent and eating food.

I didn't feel comfortable asking my parents for help because it seemed there were always strings attached to anything I received from them. I learned to "live without" from a young age. It took me many, many years to develop a better relationship with money and to let go of the "scarcity mentality" that my parents ingrained in me.

Admittedly, I still occasionally fall back into those old ways of thinking. However, I've gotten comfortable with knowing that I'm able to earn money—and I'll be able to do so one way or another as long as I need to. Money is a renewable resource, meaning it can be earned over and over again. On the other side of the coin, one can never regain the time and energy expended worrying about money. Again, it's complicated for a lot of people.

The conversation can be even more challenging if there's an imbalance between a couple when one person earns the bulk of the income. This walks me right into the story of Supported Sheila and Avoidance Arnie . . .

A Hard Talk . . .

A few months back, a couple came to me for potential planning. Theirs was a true blended family. Both had previously been married and had kids from those prior relationships. Husband Arnie, age 62, had two adult children. Wife Sheila, who was substantially younger (like, at least 25 years younger) than Arnie, had an eight-year-old daughter from a previous relationship.

Sheila was primarily a stay-at-home mom who had a self-employment side hustle that earned her very little income. Arnie had a flourishing dental practice, which he had had for 20+

years prior to the marriage. There was no prenuptial agreement between them (SMH).

Nevertheless, Arnie made it clear that he was not willing to disclose all the assets that he had or the value of his practice to anyone—let alone Sheila. I learned this ahead of our Family Wealth Planning Session (this is the name I give clients' initial estate planning meeting with me) when he left blank the asset information that I ask all prospective clients to complete on the intake forms before our initial meeting. All was left blank except information pertaining to their marital home. He had purchased their home himself but added Sheila to the title after they married. But he reiterated his refusal to reveal the extent of his asset holdings or value of his practice during our initial planning meeting. Defiant in demeanor, he was not ready to disclose to Sheila how much he made or what he was worth and simply refused to discuss it.

However, Arnie stated that he wanted to ensure his adult children received a significant portion of his estate upon his death. Sheila wanted everything from both her own and Arnie's estates to go to her and her daughter. They were definitely NOT on the same page. So much to unpack with this one!

I am not one to sit in judgment of my clients. I always tell them my office is a judgment-free zone. But clearly, money was a topic that was not freely discussed in their household—even though it really needed to be! And I told them so.

Arnie paid the bills and avoided talking about what he had. Sheila kept the household together and went along for the ride.

I ordinarily follow a fairly strict agenda at the Family Wealth Planning Session. It starts off with introductions. I discuss my firm's story, as well as how I came to leave civil litigation and transition to estate planning. I talk a lot about my "why"—while discussing a bit about myself personally, my family, my daughter, my cats, my interests, and the like. Next, I inquire about the potential clients' backgrounds and family dynamics, careers, and children. We talk about what brought them to me (their planning goals). And then I educate the clients about how the probate process works—what a Revocable Living Trust is, and so on. All of that went out the window with these two.

Instead, we spent about two hours talking about everything BUT creating their estate plan.

Undesired Consequences

True or false: For a blended family, if you are remarried, all of your assets will still pass to your biological children at your death.

FALSE!

If you have remarried and live in a Community Property State like California, and if you have no prenuptial agreement specifying to the contrary, half of your assets will automatically go to your new spouse, and the remaining half will go to your children from the prior marriage when you die without an estate plan in place. If you have remarried later in life, like Arnie, it is absolutely important to discuss this with your adult children and your new spouse in an open and understanding way.

I recommend that couples speak to each other about how each anticipates their assets would be divided at their own death, and in addition, what they expect and want to have happen as well. These may be two very different concepts, like with Arnie and Sheila. However, the couple may very well be on the same page after all. Without a substantive discussion, how is either to know? And if they are not on the same page, like Arnie and Sheila, it means it is time to talk things through before someone dies or becomes incapacitated.

I should also emphasize that any stepchildren have no right to inherit from the stepparent's estate under the law unless the intention to provide for the stepchild is part of the stepparent's plan and is put in writing. Arnie also made it clear that he did want *some* portion of his assets to go to Sheila's daughter. He did not wish to exclude her. However, he was aware that not only would Sheila take care of her daughter but so would her ex-husband, the biological father of the child. To that end, he felt justified in providing a substantial portion of his assets to his adult children, despite the fact that they had their own successful careers.

This is where the conversation was directed for Arnie and Sheila. Neither of them wanted the other to receive 50 percent of their assets upon the other's death. Regardless of this, that's exactly what would happen if they did not create and fund an estate plan that accounted for their actual desires and set them forth in a Trust.

It is not unusual for the clients to express what they specifically do not want to happen at their own death. For example, I often hear "I do not want my assets to wind up with the state . . ." or "My brother should never get a dime of my money . . ." or "I want to avoid as much in taxes as possible." But in fact, without a properly drafted, funded plan (see Chapter 8), the most undesired consequences can absolutely be the final result.

Based upon experience, I knew it was going to take several meetings to persuade Sheila that her demands were both legitimate and not reasonable. Further, Arnie's rigid way of thinking could soften if Sheila came around to understanding that Arnie's adult children would not be cut out of his estate—regardless of whether we put a plan in place or not. These are not easy conversations by any stretch of the imagination.

Ensuring that everyone is accounted for in a blended family estate plan can be very complicated. And it's so important to do it right the first time. In some ways, it isn't so hard to understand why folks like Arnie and Sheila have not yet put their estate plan in place!

At the time of this writing, I am giving Arnie and Sheila time and space to consider the reality of the situation. But it was clear that they are not there yet. I strongly suspect there will be a few more questions and conversations to be had with these two before we can begin to create their estate plan in a manner that fulfills their personal objectives. I am okay with patience as long as we keep the lines of communication open.

I am hopeful that Arnie will stop avoiding the inevitable, and that Sheila can envision receiving a smaller portion of the overall estate if Arnie is the first to die. This lawyering and counseling stuff is definitely not for wimps!

Chapter 2

Procrastinator Paul (No Need to Put Off Till Tomorrow if You're Going to Die Today)

Do you have a hard time making decisions? Are you confused about who you should give your assets to when you pass away? Are you putting off planning because you're not sure what to do? In this chapter, we'll explore how procrastination can really put a roadblock in the process for you. This chapter will show what can happen to your estate when you keep putting things off.

We all know someone like this—heck, we all have a little procrastinator in us, don't we? I'm long past due on getting that colonoscopy, but for some reason, I keep putting it off. I know I need to do it . . . and I'm going to get to it . . . really. Let's take a look at Procrastinator Paul.

For the person who failed to plan—not from fear or ignorance, but just from pure procrastination—the situation can be devastating. Over the course of my years seeing potential clients, many people have told me that the last thing they would want to happen is for their assets to wind up with the state. Failing to plan is far more relevant for people who are single, have never married (your spouse automatically becomes your power of attorney and healthcare agent), never had kids, and are without siblings.

In one such instance, I was working with an older gentleman, Paul, who had a very interesting life. He worked with NASA on the first moon landing. He developed his own line of nutritional supplements. His father had been part of the resistance in Italy during World War II. The stories he regaled me with were fascinating! But he never did get married, he had no siblings, and the only living relatives he was aware of were a couple of cousins who he thought lived in Italy. As it turned out, they had moved to the United States decades ago.

Nevertheless, we spent months poring over his assets in an attempt to locate things he'd let slip by the wayside, organize his financial papers, and come up with a distribution plan for his assets that would work for him. It also turned out that he had nearly $500,000 in stock from a previous job which he had never claimed. Any idea where that wound up?

Unclaimed Problems

Every state (as well as the federal government) has a holding place where assets are kept when no one claims them. In California, the State Controller's Office has a division referred to as the Unclaimed Property Division. The laws surrounding this topic are specific to each state, but they're similar. Overall, these laws require banks, insurance companies, and financial institutions of all kinds to report and submit certain customer information regarding unclaimed property to their State Controller's Office: property, accounts, stocks, bonds, insurance benefits, and the like.

These institutions are required to report the above when there has been no account activity for a certain period of time—generally three years. The institution will usually send out a letter, advising the owner to "claim" the property; if there is no response, the institution will be under legal obligation to turn that asset over to the state.

Now, you might think that unclaimed property must be a rare occurrence, right? WRONG!

In California, there is currently $10 billion (yep, that was a "B") in unclaimed assets sitting there, earning lots of interest for the state. I know all of you reading this just logged onto the division that deals with unclaimed property in your state to see if you can claim anything!

One more quick note here. When clients come to my office, we create an asset spreadsheet for them that lists all of the financial accounts they own. Part of the intake forms I mentioned in Chapter 1 asks the clients to provide the types of accounts and the financial institution where they are held. Whether it be a bank account, a brokerage account, an investment account, life insurance, a retirement account, or whatever type of financial assets they own—we list them, along with the name of the financial institution, including a place for identifying information (policy number, account number, etc.). This is a document we review when we meet with our clients every three years. Why? Well, we never want your assets to wind up sitting with the state.

If your successors do not know about the account and you die, that is where the asset will wind up. Life changes, your assets change—we want to ensure everything you own is accounted for (to pass on to your loved ones) and anything you no longer own is removed so that your successors aren't chasing down nonexistent accounts!

An Unfortunate Fall

Back to Paul. This man had a bit of a short-term memory issue, and he was wholly indecisive. I would call him on the phone and tell him what the plan was, according to the design we had created for his assets. Certain percentages were to be distributed to charitable institutions, some friends, creating a scholarship fund at his preferred university, and so on.

Every time I called him, he would say, "Sounds like a good plan, but I need to think about it a little bit more." I would insist that some decisions are better than no decisions and remind him that until the documents are signed, there are no decisions in place. Further, I also reminded him that we could always make changes to the plan as long as he had mental capacity.

After several months of going back and forth with him, I thought we had finally gotten to a place where he was ready for me to create the final documents. Unfortunately, before we could get those signed, Paul took a fall and died several hours later. No plan in place. At the time of this writing, the matter is proceeding through probate. Heirs whom he wasn't seemingly aware of would now be deemed beneficiaries of his estate.

In most states, if the decedent (the person who passed away) used a Will to govern distribution of their estate, then the Will needs to be submitted to the court and go through a public process called probate. Every state has its own version of probate, which is a court proceeding filed against the decedent's estate to determine the distribution of their assets based upon state law and determine who would take guardianship of any minor children. Here in California, the process is pretty horrible for a number of reasons.

Usually, the probate process requires the involvement of an attorney and does not protect the privacy of the decedent, their wishes, or their loved ones. No one is generally all that happy about hiring a lawyer.

Moreover, recall that I told you I was a trial lawyer for more than 20 years, and I can assure you that 99 percent of the people I helped with their cases over that period of time did NOT want to go to court (there are always those few strange birds who actually do want to, so I cannot legitimately say 100 percent of the people don't). Almost all want to settle OUTSIDE of court. When given the choice, most of you likely would also say "no thank you" to going to court. Therefore, it follows that your family probably doesn't want to either!

In addition, probate is a very public ordeal. Think back to almost any famous person who died . . . Prince, Aretha Franklin, Jacqueline Kennedy—and more recently, Lisa Marie Presley—to name a few. I want you to recall that there was a lot of information about their assets put out in the media. The reason for this is that a probate case is completely open to the public. This means that literally anyone (particularly the press and various types of predators) can walk into a probate court, request a copy of the filings within the file, and gain access to a list of all of the decedent's assets.

During the probate process, an administrator or executor is appointed by the court. Part of the executor's job is to "marshal"—or gather—all of the assets and have them appraised. They also create court documents that list out those assets and their values. This is so that the court can carry out one of its jobs, which is to ensure that the deceased's creditors are paid. This is how we know what many dead celebrities' estates have in terms of assets. Remember, probate is a PUBLIC proceeding, so everyone gets to look inside.

While fascinating, it is unfortunate that celebrity matters play out on a public stage. Then again, the families of celebrities are generally no strangers to the press. While most people are not super excited when "John and Susan Smith" die, their probate process is just as open and public as any celebrity's probate.

Another substantial downside is the amount of time it takes to work through the probate process. Again, every state is different, but here in California, you are looking at about 12–18 months, assuming no substantial disagreements arise, which can elongate the proceedings.

And last but not least, in California, the cost of probate is prohibitive. It is based upon the fair market value of your assets—and believe me, it is not cheap. Again, this may be different in your state.

A Revocable Living Trust avoids probate by allowing a Successor Trustee to step into the shoes of the decedent Trustee, who is usually the trustor or grantor of the Trust, and administer the Trust without court intervention or oversight.

For Procrastinator Paul, because he continued to put off the completion of his plan, this story has no happy ending. Distant relatives with whom Paul had no relationship will wind up sharing his $3 million estate, after paying the probate court, the executor of the estate, and of course, the probate lawyer. Had we not been able to locate Paul's heirs, all of Paul's assets (after any creditors were paid) would have escheated to the state.

As a side note, there are "heir finder" companies out there—companies that get paid to find the legitimate heirs of the decedent, no matter where in the world they reside. They charge a lot for these services (generally a percentage of the value of the assets, and I've seen fees around 25 percent)! Fortunately, we were able to find Paul's heirs, and we did not need to pay someone to locate them.

I encourage you to work toward removing the fear of the unexpected. Instead of worrying about what will happen when you die, I want you to be able to live your life by actually following through with your planning and getting your assets moved into your Trust with guidance from an attorney. At the end of the day, if you continuously put this off, if you procrastinate, everything you've worked toward for your entire life could wind up with people or entities that you don't even know. Don't be like Paul! His story, unfortunately, did not resolve according to his wishes . . .

Chapter 3

Clueless Cody (Live Under a Rock, and the Pressure May Kill You)

Have you thought about estate planning in the past? Do you wonder if it's something you actually need? If you don't know what an estate plan is, or why you might need one, this is the chapter for you.

Does this sound like you? It was Thursday afternoon, and 45-year-old Cody was halfway between lunch and time to leave the office for the day. There was a stack of work on his desk that needed his "immediate" attention. There were phone messages piled up that required return calls. But Cody's head was just not in the game.

Cody picked up his phone and started to scroll on Facebook. As he swiped past the litany of memes, friend posts, and cute cat pictures, Cody saw an ad or post for a "free online estate planning webinar." Cody paused for a moment and thought to himself, *Hmmm, I keep hearing that I need an estate plan. I really have no idea what that means . . . but I think it's for old people, isn't it? Something you do when you're about to die?*

This is Clueless Cody—by the way, one of my favorite types of clients!

Cody started thinking, *I'm only 45. We're not in a financial position to need an estate plan. All we have is our house, a small life insurance policy, a bit of savings, and the 401(k).*

How many times have I heard this same thing from clients? "Oh, we don't have much!" And then they proceed to list off ten different assets that would definitely have to go through probate. LOL!

Cody kept scrolling. Then, he paused for a moment. He scrolled back up. *Well, we have just been through a pandemic . . .*

Suddenly, it occurred to Cody that he knew people who'd died as a result of COVID. He wondered if they'd had an estate plan, while all the while wondering, *What is an estate plan?*

And then, he remembered a friend's cousin had just had a massive heart attack out of the blue and dropped dead at age 51!

Cody started thinking about his kids . . . *We have one child in elementary school, and one child just started middle school. What happens to my kids if something happens to my wife and to me?*

This is a common thought process which my clients relay to me all the time. Many people actually have no idea what an estate plan is or why they might actually need one—even if they are not close to death and are not über-rich

Cody decided to text his wife, Chloe. He asked her if she knew whether any of their friends had an estate plan in place, and if so, if they could they refer an attorney to contact about this. As it happens, Chloe and I are part of the same mom group on Facebook. I have helped many members of this over 10,000-member group with their estate plans, and she recalled seeing my name being recommended on a post in that group. She sent me a DM (direct message). We chatted for a few minutes and scheduled a Family Wealth Planning Session for later that same month.

Now, there's a reason I said that Clueless Cody is one of my favorite types of clients. When he and Chloe came into my office for their planning session, he had no preconceived notions about what estate planning was or how it would benefit his family. Fortunately, neither of them had had to deal with the loss of a parent or close relative, and they were completely oblivious to the process of passing assets or designating guardians. Cody was a blank slate, waiting for me to educate him about what he did not know.

When push comes to shove, I am all about educating people about the ins and outs of estate planning, probate, and how to keep families out of court and out of conflict. In fact, I often give educational seminars on estate planning and Kid Protection Planning® for parent resource groups, single-mom groups, financial planners, and so on, just to help educate my community about this stuff. It is that important! Because the truth is, I'm just one attorney—I cannot help everyone in the entire community. In fact, I actually limit the number of new clients I take on each month in order to be able to provide a high level of service to each of them. With that said, having a bit of knowledge and information—even if a family does not come to me for planning—my hope is that I can provide an understanding of how estate planning can give them peace of mind while they are alive about what will happen when they pass away.

Harking back to the introduction about what an estate plan is and why YOU need one, we can take a look at Cody's situation and use his circumstances as an example of what can happen if no plan is in place, and in the alternative, how things actually were different because Cody and Chloe came to my office and put their plan into place. Hopefully, this will help, and it will become crystal clear.

Designating the Primary Beneficiary

In looking at Cody and Chloe's financial situation, they were in pretty good shape, all things considered. They owned a home (with a mortgage); they each had a modest life insurance policy; of course, they had a couple of checking accounts, savings accounts, a small brokerage account; they had started 529 college savings plans for their two kids. Cody also had a decent 401(k) with contributions from his employer. All in all, their assets totaled about $3.5 million, the bulk of that being the value of their home. (You know how it is in California—even a small shack in a good neighborhood goes for at least $1 million!)

Now, you may recall that when I discussed probate in Chapter 2, I mentioned that the cost in each state is different. But here in California, where I practice, it averages out to 5 percent of the fair market value of the assets owned. The probate court does not care if there is a mortgage balance—that is not how the costs and fees are determined. So, for Cody and Chloe, if we look beyond the potential issues of not planning to just the cost we're talking about $175,000 for the judge to determine who raises the kids, who Cody and Chloe's creditors are and how much they get and ultimately who gets the balance of the assets (the kids when they turn 18). Who wants to throw $175,000 down the drain? No one I know.

And I can promise you this: while I'm neither the cheapest nor the most expensive in terms of the fees I charge to create a comprehensive estate plan, the cost is nowhere near $175,000! Not even in the same ballpark!

Another key element in getting an estate plan in place has to do with naming beneficiaries on certain types of accounts, like retirement accounts and life insurance that are actually passed outside of a Trust. These types of accounts have a specific designated beneficiary, where the owner of the account informs the company holding the asset who is to receive those funds when the owner dies. One of the things that a nontraditional estate planning attorney (me) does is guide clients about how to designate beneficiaries to achieve the stated and desired goals. That can even mean naming the Trust itself as the primary beneficiary!

Let's look at a couple of different potential scenarios. Imagine, if you will, Cody initially listed his wife as the primary beneficiary and his minor kids as the backup beneficiaries on his 401(k) retirement account. If Cody and Chloe die together, that retirement account is destined to go through probate (even if they created a Trust). Why? Because a minor cannot own a financial asset. (We will talk more about that in Chapter 4.) If the minor children are designated as the backup beneficiaries (instead of a Trust), that retirement account asset winds up in probate.

What if Cody designated his younger brother as the beneficiary because he never got around to changing his designation forms after he and Chloe got married? Believe me when I tell you, people often forget to change over their designations! On multiple occasions, clients have told me that they actually had no idea who they had designated on their beneficiary forms, or worse, that they did not designate anyone! Once Cody dies, there is no changing that beneficiary form. So, in this scenario, Cody's younger brother gets all that hard-earned retirement money, leaving Chloe and the kids without recourse because a beneficiary designation will dictate who gets the asset—despite contradictory terms in a Trust!

Please note: there may be a potential argument for Chloe that California is a Community Property State, and therefore she is entitled to the community property interests in that retirement account, but this would likely be a question for the probate or family law court.

And what if Cody's younger brother has a disability and receives financial, need-based government benefits such as Supplemental Security Income (SSI)? When the 401(k) is inherited, Cody's younger brother will most likely lose those government benefits if they are, in fact, need-based and require financial eligibility.

And finally, what about the unlikely but still possible scenario of Cody, Chloe, and their two kids all passing away together? In that scenario, the court will have no choice but to determine who Cody and Chloe's "heirs" are—based upon state law. In case you don't already know, an heir is a person who may legally receive property or assets from a deceased person's estate when there is no Will or Trust in place. That could mean Cody's younger brother (who is disabled and receives need-based government benefits) would likely inherit a portion of the estate, causing him to lose those benefits.

Do you think Cody was aware of any of this when he and Chloe came to my office? Nope, he had no idea. Clueless Cody was not so clueless after spending a couple of hours with me!

Not So Clueless Now!

Truth be told, I could probably run another ten scenarios with the different potential pitfalls of Cody and Chloe not understanding what could happen because they did not have a plan in place, including having no say in who would be given guardianship of their kids . . . but I know you are catching on to how this works.

The good news is that Cody and Chloe worked with me to establish their Revocable Living Trust. They decided whom they would want to raise their kids in the event that something happens to both of them while their kids are still minors, and we created an entire Kid Protection Plan®. I also provided guidance about how to designate beneficiaries on their life insurance and their retirement accounts so that their priorities and goals would be met upon their demise. And Cody's brother, designated as a contingent (or backup) beneficiary, would not lose his government benefits if any funds were designated to come his way, because they would be passed via a Supplemental Needs Trust rather than an outright distribution. Welcome to those in the know, Cody.

Maybe there is something to this estate planning stuff. And just maybe, like Cody, you need to think about it right now!

Chapter 4

The Story of Meager Melanie (So, You Thought You Had Nothing to Lose . . .)

Are you of the mindset that you don't have a lot of financial assets to give to anyone when you die? Do you believe that a close family member will automatically be chosen to raise your minor child at your death? In this chapter, we're going to look at the three primary reasons you might need a plan and why leaving it up to a court to decide who raises your child is not the best option.

Let's see if this sounds at all familiar . . . Melanie and her husband, Mike, are a middle-aged couple with one daughter. They don't own a home; they rent the house that they've lived in for the last five years. Mike is currently unemployed (and by currently, I mean for the last seven years). He'd been a stay-at-home dad (a wannabe entertainer) since their daughter, Annabelle, was born. Melanie works a full-time job and makes a decent salary, but she brings home barely enough to pay the bills and afford Annabelle some extracurricular activities.

They live a modest life and don't have much in savings or retirement accounts. It's on their to-do list, that is, to save enough money to be able to retire someday, but they're not there yet. They live pretty much paycheck to paycheck and have hopes and dreams that someday they'll be able to buy a place of their own. It's on Melanie's mind that she and Mike need to plan for what happens if something happens to them. At the same time, Mike's of the mindset that they don't have anything anyway—so what do they need to plan for?

In my experience, moms tend to think, worry, and obsess about this substantially more than dads do. Mike figures that if they kick the bucket, a family member will take in Annabelle and hopefully have enough money to take care of her until she's an adult. Honestly, there's a litany of issues that arise from that thought process . . .

Meanwhile, Melanie wrestles with competing concepts. On one hand, she feels like they need to make a plan; on the other hand, it seems like they have barely any assets at all . . . so why do they need a plan?

Do I Really Need This, Though?

Let me start by saying that in my office we have a philosophy that if you have any one of these things, then you really need to create an estate plan:

1. Real estate

2. Minor children
3. Total assets that exceed the threshold for your state's laws for probate*

***NOTE:** It's different in every state, but here in California that figure was $184,500 in 2023.

Without an estate plan, you're leaving it up to a court to decide who gets your property, who raises your children, and how your assets are divided. This is how it works! Either you create a legal plan for yourself—with the help of a lawyer!—setting forth to whom, and when, you want your assets to go when you die, and who you would want to raise your minor children. Alternatively, a judge will decide for you.

There really is no other option. You volunteer to let the courts distribute your cash and personal stuff—or you decide to take control of your own decision-making and plan. When you fail to handle this for yourself, every state has its own version of the court process known as probate to deal with these issues instead. (Probate, as more fully discussed in Chapter 2, is a court process for the distribution of assets and guardianship for minors according to laws in your state.) Even if you have limited assets, there is still a court process, albeit shorter in duration, to distribute your assets when you die.

In Melanie and Mike's case, they have a minor child, so they qualify on that basis alone under my firm's philosophy for needing an estate plan. That's because if they don't set forth their desires (in a legal document) as to whom they want to raise their child in the event something happens to them, a judge would make the decision about where their child would live and who would raise her. Melanie and Mike would have absolutely no say in the matter.

Less Is Less, Until It's More

There are so many different ways this can go wrong, but in Chapter 7 I'll be diving into the family who fails to take steps to protect their child. But focusing solely on the limited financial assets that Melanie and Mike do have, although they don't think that they have much, they met the criteria for number 3 above. Before they came to meet with me in my office, Melanie and Mike filled out some intake forms on which they indicated having several life insurance policies as well as a savings account that put them just over the $184,500 in total assets mark. They had named their daughter, a minor child, as the beneficiary of those life insurance policies.

So, let's just say for example, Melanie and Mike did nothing . . .

- They didn't come to my office.
- They didn't seek to create a plan for their assets.
- They didn't set up guardianships for their child.

And then one or both of them died . . .

By listing the minor child as the beneficiary on life insurance policies, this guarantees a court being involved. This is because a minor child cannot own a financial asset. Think about going to a bank to open up a savings account for your child. If your child is under 18, the bank wouldn't allow just the child's name to be on the account. You would need to be the custodian of that account. The same is true of any financial asset, whether it be the proceeds of life insurance, a brokerage, or bank account.

When a child is named as a beneficiary, someone must determine what happens to that money until the child turns 18. I'll give you one guess as to who that might be! Yup . . . it's going to be a judge. The judge has to follow the law of your state and open a blocked (meaning no access to the funds) guardianship account set up and put the money in it. The child will not get to use the money until they turn 18. Then your child will get all of the money from that blocked account in one shot.

Whether the amount of money is $184,500 or $10,845,000, there is no guidance, nothing, that tells the 18-year-old what to do with that money. And there are no restrictions on what they can do with it. Not an ideal approach, am I right?

Fortunately, Melanie's inner voice got the best of her. They did come to my office to discuss putting together an estate plan. And I explained to them that one of my goals is to keep their family out of court when something happens to them. We created a Revocable Living Trust in order that their assets would be used to take care of their daughter until she could support herself. As Melanie and Mike acquire more assets, which they will, they want to ensure that their daughter isn't having to rely upon the kindness of other family members to pay for her upbringing.

As parents, it's our job to have the finances to support our children until they are able to support themselves. When I met with Melanie and Mike, we talked, among other topics, about how their life insurance could be increased. They were already paying for several small policies, but it made much more sense for them to increase the value of those policies while they were still young and could afford to do so. This was done to provide the financial resources Annabelle would need until she was capable of working and earning a living.

It is also important to note that when considering who to name as guardians, you should NOT be thinking about whether that person (or couple) has sufficient funds to take care of your kid(s)! It is our responsibility as parents to financially provide for the child(ren)—we cannot place that burden on the guardians. In fact, it is a very common mistake that people make when considering guardians. But I'm here to tell you, it doesn't matter what the potential guardian has—YOU need to provide the monetary support for the care and raising of your child(ren). Maybe that means increasing the value of the life insurance policy or trying to save a little extra each month in your rainy-day fund.

Imagine if you were designated as a guardian for someone's child and then expected not only to raise that child but to pay for them as well! It costs a lot of money to raise a child to adulthood, and don't forget, your initial choice could say no—especially if they do not have the means! According to Investopedia and statistics from the Brookings Institute (an economic think tank), the average middle-income family will spend $310,605 to raise a child born in 2015 to age 17![2] I'm not sure that most people have an extra $310,000 lying around to raise your child.

Welcome to Have-a-Lot!

By creating a Trust, Melanie and Mike can rest assured that Annabelle would have guidance on how to use money left to her via a Trust with the people they chose as potential Successor Trustees. A Successor Trustee is the person, persons, or institution selected by the one making the Trust to take over the management of assets in the Living Trust when they die or become incapacitated. The Successor Trustee is designated to take care of the assets and carry out the stated distribution or instructions within the Trust.

Instead of listing Annabelle, a minor, as the beneficiary of those life insurance policies, we named their Trust as the beneficiary. By doing so, the proceeds would pass into the Trust (to

2 "How Much Does It Cost to Raise a Child in the U.S.?" by Tim Parker, updated May 3, 2023, Investopedia—Dotdash Meredith publishing family (Online Article)

be used to take care of Annabelle), alleviating the need for a court process. Again, if a minor is named as the beneficiary, the court *must* step in and hold that financial asset until the minor reaches the age of majority.

So, now Melanie and Mike know that whatever funds are left will not be turned over to Annabelle when she turns 18. This means peace of mind while they're both still alive and a future where their daughter thrives without them if need be. They may have believed they were of meager means, but they hit the jackpot when they put their plan in place!

Chapter 5

Apathetic Andy (100 Percent Mortality, Whether You Care or Not)

Have you ever thought that estate planning is unnecessary because you'll be dead and don't really care what happens once you are gone? Does creating an estate plan really matter for you, since you will be dead when it comes into play? This story reveals how personal life circumstances may have you thinking twice about not caring what happens to your assets after you die.

Andy and Allison, an older couple, came into my office a few years ago, looking to do an estate plan. Well, actually it was Allison who was looking to do an estate plan. She basically dragged her husband along, as is often the case in my practice. I'm not exactly sure why it is generally the wife and mother who is the driving force behind taking those initial steps to get the estate plan done, but it is very common in my practice. Kind of a reverse "ball and chain."

As is customary, I began the meeting by talking a little bit about myself and my practice, my process, and why I do what I do. Then I began to inquire about Andy and Allison.

Let me stop here for a second and explain: when someone comes to my office, they have already filled out a set of intake forms (referenced in Chapter 1), which helps inform me a little bit about them and their planning goals. Regardless, I don't dive into establishing a plan with them when they first come into my office. I'm not a fan of that "Wham bam, let's do your plan" type of lawyering.

Part of my process involves talking for a while: explaining who I am, why I do what I do, building trust. A relationship with a lawyer (as well as with many other professionals) relies on a foundation of trust. It is my belief that trust can be built during that initial conversation if the potential clients get a sense of what I'm truly about in terms of my desire to help people, my background, and my being transparent about the way I got to where I am today.

I also spend time getting to know the clients, to understand their family dynamic and really diving into the heart of why they came to me for estate planning. By the time they arrive in my office, most people know, either consciously or subconsciously, that they want to get their plan done, that they need to get their plan done; they're just not really sure about all the particulars. To help them feel comfortable with me and the concept of estate planning, we have to talk about where they are coming from and where they hope to go.

Sitting with Andy and Allison in my office, I began asking questions about their background and their kids. I asked them to give me broad brushstrokes about their upbringing, relationships, schooling, career choices, and how they met each other. Allison told me that her dad was a minister from New York but had moved to California to run his own parish. She grew up in a very religious household, and she attended a Bible college before transferring to UCLA (GO BRUINS!).

She had a close-knit family, with a couple of brothers and sisters. She had enjoyed a happy childhood, although she did not come from a lot of wealth. The church played a significant role in her upbringing. In fact, she met Andy when she was 22 at a church retreat and instantly fell in love—although she didn't let him know that! They were married two years later. Allison got her teaching credentials and taught middle and high school Spanish. Later, when she had her two children in the early 1970s, she never returned to teaching but stayed busy volunteering at the church and doing odd jobs.

Andy spoke next. He told me a bit about his background. He was born in Oklahoma, but while he was still a toddler, his family moved to California. His dad had owned several gas stations in the Banning area. Andy was drafted into the army in the early 1960s. He was in the military for the required time, then got out of the army to study engineering. He had always been interested in surveying and went to work for the county government. By the time we met in my office, he had been retired for more than 15 years. He had his pension, a decent amount of savings, and a house that was fully paid off.

At this point in the conversation, I asked them about their intentions. Why were they here in my office? And what is it that they hoped to accomplish with their planning? Allison started off by saying that one of their children had some challenges. This naturally sparked my curiosity, but I allowed her to continue her thoughts without interruption. She said that she was hopeful that she and Andy could plan things out so that things would pass to their children without having to go through any court process.

Having already lost their parents, they reflected that only Allison's folks had done any sort of planning. Andy's parents had not, and there had been a probate proceeding. This was something Allison knew she wanted to avoid for the sake of her children.

What Do I Care . . . ?

By this time, my curiosity had gotten the better of me, and I asked Allison about her adult children. Their daughter, Theresa, was a gem: married for 23 years, two adult daughters in college, very close with Allison and Andy. They could not say enough good things about this one! Then, there was the "challenged" child, their son, Ernest: in his early 50s, still living at home, divorced, and . . . facing a substantial drinking problem. Oh, and he would spend money that he didn't have because he collected government benefits due to his obsessive-compulsive disorder—he could not hold down a job. Oh boy.

I then turned to Andy to get his take on things. It was at this point that Andy said something to me that I hear relatively infrequently—but I have heard it before, almost exclusively from men. It's a little shocking to hear at first, but when discussing his intentions for their planning, he point-blank answered, in a rather matter-of-fact manner, "What do I care? I'll be dead."

Whoa! Did he really just say that? I couldn't believe my ears.

My thoughts started racing, and I had to take a few deep breaths to try to formulate how to address this indifferent point of view. First, I asked him if he was truly being serious with that statement. All the while, I was thinking . . . *Does he really not care if his alcoholic son drinks away all of Andy's hard-earned money?* Was he prepared for Ernest to lose his government benefits because of a substantial inheritance? Was he oblivious to the effect this would have on Theresa when Ernest blew through his share of the funds and started harassing his sister for some portion of her share of the estate?

In case you are wondering, I have seen similar situations—where parents leave equal portions of their estate to their adult children, one of whom has a drug, alcohol, or gambling problem. That adult child inevitably wastes their entire inheritance on <fill in addiction here> and then turns to the sibling(s) for bailout. It never ends well for the "responsible child" who generally gets sucked into the vortex of the addict.

With these thoughts in mind, I decided I needed to appeal to Andy's military background and even the structure of his work as an engineer. His son was bringing unruly chaos to their lives. Ernest's lifestyle and challenges could very well undo all of Andy's hard work and legacy.

The Power of Trustee

One of the truly beautiful things about estate planning is that more often than not, there's a solution for whatever problem presents itself to the issues raised within the family's dynamic. In this case, Andy and Allison knew that, without them present, their adult alcoholic son could not manage any sum of money—regardless of whether he was drinking, sober, or somewhere in between. They also did not want to burden their responsible daughter with "babysitting" Ernest for the rest of their lives.

For this reason, I was able to propose a plan that included never actually **giving** the money or other assets to Ernest. Rather, the plan was for **holding** those assets in trust with a money manager—or Successor Trustee. They would then **use** the money to provide ongoing health care, education, maintenance, and support to Ernest (at the discretion of the Successor Trustee) for as long as his share of those assets would last. And fortunately, Andy and Allison had sufficient assets that Ernest would likely never outlive his share of his parents' estate if it were properly managed.

At the end of the day, Andy actually did see the error in his way of thinking. I believe that he was so frustrated with his adult son's lifestyle that Andy basically threw in the proverbial towel. His "I'll be dead, what do I care?" attitude was his defense mechanism for not knowing what else to do. He didn't see a way to help his alcoholic son get over his addiction.

Simultaneously, Andy didn't want Ernest to be on the streets. He didn't want Ernest to completely drain his share of the money. And he certainly did not want to saddle Theresa and her husband with having to bail Ernest out after he drank through his entire share of the estate.

I am happy to report that we set up Andy and Allison's Trust plan to ensure that Theresa would get her share without having to worry about Ernest harassing her for additional money. Not only that, but we also set Ernest up with a Successor Trustee who will work to ensure Ernest's in-budget expenses are paid, he has a place to live, and he is taken care of in a way that the money his parents left him will last throughout his lifetime.

We gave the Successor Trustee the power to monitor Ernest's discretionary spending and even drug/alcohol test him if they feel it is necessary before doling out unbudgeted cash to Ernest. Ernest will never actually be in control of his inheritance. There will always be an independent Successor Trustee to stand in the place of Andy and Allison. No matter how dreadful the future may seem in this scenario, WIN-WINs are still possible!

Chapter 6

A Tale of Two Clients: Skeptical Sue and Isolated Irwin (To Trust or Not to Trust . . . Is That Really the Question?)

Among other reasons, have you not gotten your estate plan in place because you are not sure who you can trust to handle the responsibilities? Perhaps you do not have close family members or even friends you believe you can rely on to deal with the carrying out of your own decisions? The avatars in this chapter are in similar, yet different, circumstances. Neither has that "go-to" person who can deal with the incapacity and post-death responsibilities. Here, I'll show you how these issues can be dealt with.

Right off the top, this scenario is a little hard for me to relate to—allow me to check my privilege with you. Personally, I am fortunate to be married and have a child; to have a sibling, nieces, and nephews, along with many cousins with whom I'm close; and to have a group of close friends and colleagues. If something were to happen to me, in addition to all of these folks I have around me, there are also several charities near and dear to my heart. But I recognize there are many people out there who do not have the benefit of having close family members around them, or who may not have ties to any philanthropic organizations.

That established, I will now share the stories of Skeptical Sue and Isolated Irwin. They are similar yet different . . .

Isolated Irwin

When Irwin came to me, he relayed his story. He had been married, but his wife had passed away 10 years earlier. After marrying the love of his life, he had 30 years of "blissful" marriage to her before her death from cancer. Their life together sounded magical—but, of course, the sentimentality of his recollection lacked darker elements of the truth.

Irwin's wife had the good fortune of making excellent business decisions and invested her time, energy, and attention into building several successful businesses. In fact, she was the bread earner in the family. She established relationships with partners whom she trusted, who took over running the businesses entirely once she was diagnosed with cancer and continued doing so after her death. As it turned out, the cancer was extremely aggressive, and she survived for only about two months after her diagnosis. Needless to say, this left Irwin devastated. He was still devastated ten years later.

During both of their lifetimes, those lucrative businesses that Irwin's wife developed, nurtured, and grew afforded them the luxury of travel to tropical destinations—all first-class accommodations and the best in wining and dining. They lived in an amazing condominium in Hermosa Beach, walking distance from the water. They had all of the comforts, toys, gadgets, electronics, and everything a person with unlimited funds might consider acquiring.

In addition, they owned several properties—all prosperous rentals that did not carry mortgages. Irwin ended up receiving about $12 million in assets—including cash, businesses, real property, retirement accounts, and brokerage accounts after his wife passed away.

Irwin and his wife never did have children. From his description, they were too busy enjoying life to be tied down to raising kids. They had cats!

In addition, Irwin was an only child. His wife had a brother and a sister, nieces, nephews, and some cousins, all of whom lived within the same state but hundreds of miles away. Given the fact that from north to south, California is over 1,000 miles at its longest, this isn't difficult to picture. Short of Irwin and his wife traveling to them for family events, holidays, and the like, they did not see much of that side of the family.

Irwin explained that he tolerated these people but did not have a close relationship with them. He believed they maintained a relationship with his wife because she had abundant wealth. He said, "They often had their hands out to ask us for money when things got tough, as if we were some kind of money vending machine." (Otherwise known as an ATM.) I sensed some bitterness in his tone. Apparently, once his wife died (and all of her wealth was transferred to him), her family members basically abandoned him. Occasionally, he would call his wife's family to say hello, but those calls were rarely reciprocated.

Irwin and his wife did have an estate plan in place, and there clearly was not a lot of thought put into planning from the standpoint of designating multiple levels of fiduciaries—in case the primary would not or could not serve, and the couple had basically only named each other and one backup. Also, there was no business succession plan for all of the wife's business interests. So, Irwin was referred to me by a mutual acquaintance to update his Trust and ancillary documents and to figure out what to do with all of the assets he had inherited.

He really had no clue about the businesses and was grateful that the business partners handled the ongoing day-to-day running of the business, paying the employees, and keeping the businesses profitable. Those partners also provided him with accounting reports and spreadsheets about the business (which he did not really understand) and, of course, a monthly income. While Irwin may not have understood the inner workings of the businesses, he was savvy enough to know that SOMETHING needed to be determined about his deceased wife's shares when something happened to him.

The problem for Irwin was, he really had no idea what to do with all of these acquired holdings. He had no family members of his own. He wasn't overly fond of his wife's family. But he knew in his heart of hearts that she would have wanted to take care of them with some portion of all that money—particularly her nieces and nephews, who she felt were good people, despite their parents' disconnect. He felt totally isolated. Almost like he was back on one of those tropical islands he and his wife visited annually, but without the warm and fuzzy feelings that went along with the vacation.

Skeptical Sue

Sue was a 40-year-old single mom with an infant child; she had previously moved to California from Vermont to go to college and pursue a music career. She was professionally trained but never quite seemed to "make it" in the competitive world of classical musicians. Her mother had died when she was a young child. Her relationship with her father was strained because he was intent on controlling her life and telling her how to live it. Moreover, he had not been around much during her childhood, choosing instead to focus on work and earning money to pay for the nanny he hired to raise his children. Her father did not approve of Sue's artistic side and desire to earn a living in "the arts."

Sue had a younger brother who, upon attaining adulthood, was similarly controlling in his relationship with his own wife and children. During their formative years, Sue's father had sown the seeds of contention between Sue and her younger brother. So, when it came time to head out of state for college, Sue easily disengaged from her entire family without batting an eye.

Sue would speak with her father on only an inconsistent basis until he suddenly passed away in the fall of 2022, leaving her brother in charge of the probate in their home state. Prior to his death, Sue's dad had provided Sue some ongoing financial support to supplement the odd jobs and private tutoring lessons she gave. This was at least part of the reason she did not cut him off from her life completely.

When Sue came to me, she was aware that she would be inheriting about $4 million in assets from her father's estate, although she suspected it might have been more if someone other than her brother were in charge of the estate. She had already received some life insurance funds, which she used to support herself and her infant child while on maternity leave. She was anxiously awaiting the resolution of the probate so she could receive her inheritance. Even though her father never did understand or accept Sue's decision to become a single parent by choice, he clearly loved her in the best way he could (even if not in the way she wanted or needed). This was somewhat evident in the fact that he had ensured there were plenty of assets to take care of her (and her child) for the long haul.

The problem was that Sue's father had put her brother in charge of the money by naming him as the executor of the Will. Sue's father did not create a Trust for his assets in Vermont; he merely created a Will. As such, you know what's coming . . . his estate had to go through probate. Sue found out about this when she received notification from her brother's lawyer that a probate had been opened. Sue's brother didn't even have the courtesy to give her a call to inform her of what was going on. Sue had to hire her own Vermont lawyer to protect her rights in the probate proceedings. Sue and her brother had not spoken since she received that notice in the mail.

For reasons unknown to me, Sue did not have many close ties with friends nor with any of her family members on either her mother's or father's side of the family. She didn't even maintain friendships with people she had known from when she lived in Vermont. She had lived in California for a number of years and had some friends and acquaintances, but she wasn't sure if she trusted any of them enough to name them as a fiduciary to handle the substantial funds she inherited from her father when she eventually passed away. She was truly skeptical of those around her.

Who Can Handle the Job?

Here are two people, Irwin and Sue, who have completely different background stories. However, they found themselves in similar predicaments in terms of selecting trustworthy fiduciaries to handle their affairs following death. Irwin was basically alone in the world. Sue, while she had family, did not have a relationship with them—and was doubtful that she could trust her friends with the amount of money she inherited. And her son was only a baby.

Irwin's and Sue's situations are often a challenge for estate planning attorneys. I, for one, would not feel comfortable telling anyone what they SHOULD do in this situation. The job of the estate planner is to provide guidance and options and to lay out how each choice would likely play out in the long term. Ultimately, the decision about what to do is up to the person doing their own planning.

Sue's situation was actually somewhat easier, since she was open to using either a financial institution (a bank) or a licensed professional fiduciary to manage her assets after her death, until her child was old enough to take over. As a fiduciary, a bank's primary duty is the management and care of property for others. Most banks and financial institutions have a division that undertakes these types of services and responsibilities on behalf of people who wish to designate them as such. Banks do tend to charge more for these services than a licensed professional fiduciary—but in some instances, such as Sue's, a bank is a good option.

I was able to structure Sue's Trust and estate plan in a way that gave her peace of mind that her assets would be well taken care of and managed to her specifications, primarily to support her son. When he turns a certain age of her choosing, he will receive the balance of the funds left in trust. Moreover, within Sue's Trust document, we designated an attorney (me) to assist her child in his dealings with the financial institution—in addition to naming guardians to take care of him in the event of Sue's death.

Sue's skepticism was assuaged when I showed her how we could manage her estate in a way that made sense to her. I conveyed to Sue that the financial institution and professional fiduciary she chose to safeguard her assets had professional expertise in managing assets and administering Trusts—including knowledgeable and experienced personnel. Further, I explained that banks have systems in place to safeguard the assets under their management and robust internal controls, and they are subject to regulatory oversight—which can provide an additional layer of protection for the assets of a Trust. Sue was no longer skeptical!

In contrast, Irwin was not open to having a financial institution, corporate entity, or someone he didn't know manage his money. In order to help him make decisions in this regard, we walked through an exercise that I use with clients who face similar challenges in selecting fiduciaries. What it boils down to is coming up with a list of people the client believes are capable of handling the job. Next, based upon who is on that list, I suggest the client think about which of those people tend to make the same kind of decisions around money that the client does.

For example, if the client has a high tolerance for investment risk, they should probably not choose someone who is super conservative in their attitude toward money and investing. After several discussions, Irwin was able to designate one of his wife's business advisors as his primary fiduciary and chose a friend who is an accountant as the backup.

I could probably write an entire chapter on Irwin's decisions, indecisions, and changes in terms of the friends, charities, and wife's family members he decided to leave cash gifts to—but this still is an ongoing saga. Regardless, Irwin wound up not quite as isolated as he originally thought. And while we could not bring his wife back, we absolutely honored her hard work while taking care to ensure Irwin's peace of mind.

Chapter 7

DIY David (Who Wants to Assemble Their Trust from Ikea?)

Are you the type who, at a minimum, will try to do most things on your own rather than seeking out a professional? Have you ever tried to fill out an online form to deal with a legal matter? In this chapter, we will look at why the DIY of legal documents can leave your loved ones with a big hot mess.

Honestly, this is the one excuse for which I have the least amount of patience. Here is the story of DIY (do it yourself) David.

There was a younger couple in their early 30s, David and Delia. They had two very young children under the age of four. One day, David decided to log on to one of the DIY legal form websites (like legalzoom.com, willmaker.com, trustandwill.com, or nolo.com) to see about creating a Will and maybe a Trust. David began to navigate around on the site and thought to himself, *Okay I can do this. How hard can it be?*

Stopping here for a second, I wish I had been there to whisper into his ear. So I'll whisper into yours instead. You may not be aware of this, but in most states, lawyers not only have to get a four-year university degree, they also spend an additional three years in law school. Following law school, they must pass a rigorous multi-day examination in order to practice law.

In other words, there is a great deal of time, energy, and effort put forth in becoming a lawyer. Perhaps some of you were not aware of that. The point is that practicing law is not something to be taken lightly. It requires dedication, analytical and logical thinking skills, problem-solving skills, research skills, attention to detail, and knowledge of complex statutes (laws) to name a few of the skills necessary.

Back to the mindset of "surely, it can't be that hard to fill out some forms online!" Well . . . creating an estate plan is not the same as browsing an internet marketplace, filling your cart, and clicking "checkout." There are i's to dot, t's to cross, and legal matters that may sneak by you.

So, I don't want to sound like I'm on my high horse here, but this is one that really gets to me. I want to carefully address the idea that people are smart enough to figure this stuff out for themselves. There is no question that many people can fill out the forms. They can follow the instructions offered on the website. They can, in fact, get a set of documents from the website.

That is to say, writing your own Will and thinking that you're doing the right thing by your family can lead to a false sense of security, believing that the DIY was sufficient. Let me ask you DIYers to contemplate some things . . .

If you broke your leg, you wouldn't try to set it yourself, would you? I'm guessing you'd go to a hospital, or at the very least, to an orthopedic surgeon. Yeah?

When you have a toothache due to a cavity, you don't start drilling in your own mouth to fill that cavity, do you? (Unless you are Tom Hanks in that movie *Cast Away*, and you are on a deserted island with nothing but a rock to cure that toothache—ouch! It pains me just thinking about that scene!)

If something is wrong with the plumbing, have you learned to let go and let the expert handle it? If you are anything like my husband, you might watch YouTube videos and think that you can repair the kitchen sink faucet. Most often, you'll likely find, in the long run, that you didn't do it right. Now the leak is worse, so you wind up calling a plumber, after having to shut the water off for two days. But I digress.

Truly, I get it. Times are tough. Money is tight. But what most people, especially the DIYers, don't understand is that when you do estate planning wrong, it winds up costing your family and your own estate potentially tens of thousands—maybe even hundreds of thousands—of dollars more than it would have had you gone to a competent estate planning attorney in the first place.

Some Things Should Just Be Left to a Professional!

Why, you ask? I mean, don't legalzoom.com, nolo.com, and similar sites exist for a reason? They do, and there may be some decent applications (obviously, I have some bias here) for which they can save a person some expense. I personally do not have experience checking out every application these sites offer.

However, I have reviewed many DIY documents produced from these types of sites. And just like with David and Delia, there are substantial consequences when you try to DIY. Inevitably, it comes out DIWrong.

There are many aspects to the DIWrong. First, the DIY sites do not provide LEGAL ADVICE, because they can't. The site is not a lawyer, and only a lawyer can provide legal advice (every state has its own version of California's unauthorized practice of law, or UPL, which is a misdemeanor, according to CA Business & Professions Code sections 6125, 6126).

Additionally, the site cannot tell you what documents you may actually need for your plan—those sites can only offer a variety of different documents that may or may not be what you need for YOUR family. Further, those sites cannot provide guidance as to how to choose the appropriate fiduciaries that you may need to designate, depending upon which documents you are creating. Moreover, the site cannot discuss (anything) with you regarding whether a Will is appropriate, whether a Trust is appropriate—or maybe whether both are needed. And what about incapacity planning? How is that different from end-of-life planning? None of them offer the Kid Protection Planning® that my office provides.

By doing this on your own, you are taking a substantial risk that not only do you DIWrong, but you will likely have a false sense of security that you have actually protected your family because you filled out the forms!

It is possible that these consequences are potentially not going to affect you—well . . . because you'll be dead. However, the whole point of estate planning is to take care of things the way you would want them to go and to protect the people you love who survive you. And when you do it wrong, not only do you leave your family with a mess, but it can be a very expensive, drawn-out mess.

What do I mean? Well, in the state of California, as noted previously in Chapter 4, if you have assets that exceed $184,500 (this figure relates solely to California and is subject to annual changes based on inflation pursuant to the California Probate Code) or you have real property such as a house or a condominium, these assets can only pass to your loved ones through the court process (probate) unless you have a comprehensive estate plan. Also, in California, pre-pandemic, it took between 12 and 18 months to get through probate (this is for the state of California; each state has its own probate process). During that time, your family is in court, and all of your assets are tied up (meaning, they cannot be used by your family at a time they would likely need them), waiting for a judge to determine what, if anything, goes to your creditors and then who gets the balance. Added to that, if you have minor children, they could wind up in foster care for some period of time while the court determines who should become their guardian.

Sit with this thought for a moment. If something happens to you, who determines what happens to your minor children? A judge. What happens between the time something happens to you and the judge appointing a guardian? Keep in mind, nothing happens quickly in the court setting—even an emergency court hearing requires 24-hour notice.

During the interim time between an accident or something happening to you and someone stepping forward in a court setting to accept guardianship of the minor children, those kids have been placed with a foster family by the Department of Child & Family Services (DCFS). And what if you are not dead but merely incapacitated? That DIY Will, which might list a potential guardian, does not even come into play until you have died. This leaves zero guidance for a judge to help determine who should take care of your minor children until you regain capacity.

And then there is the expense. In California, the cost of probate will run your estate around 5 percent of the fair market value of all of your combined assets. Believe me when I tell you, no plan created by my office is going to cost anywhere near 5 percent of the value of your assets!

Granted, estate planning fees will change over time, including mine, but I offer different levels of planning for the client to choose which options best fit their family's needs. I work with clients on payment plans if they require a little more time to pay. I may not be as cheap as DIY, but you get what you pay for—and I'm confident the plans created by my office are going to work when they are needed. Can't say the same for DIY!

Problems Without Signatures

Getting back to David and Delia . . . when they came to me, they had filled out the family inventory and assessment forms ahead of our planning session. Their responses indicated the following:

- They owned a house with an estimated fair market value of $1,400,000.
- They had bank accounts and investment accounts that exceeded $50,000.
- They had life insurance in the amount of $2 million.
- They had about $150,000 in retirement accounts.

Without even taking into account the value of their vehicles, home furnishings, jewelry, and other items within their home, the probate (court process) in their case would have cost more than $180,000. David and Delia also brought to me their DIY documents from one of those aforementioned online sites. Can I tell you that not only were those forms a total disaster, but the couple had not even SIGNED them!

So, the few hundred dollars David spent to create those (worthless) documents was completely wasted because David and Delia hadn't even taken the most basic of required steps when it comes to practically any type of legal document. Documents have to be signed, often witnessed, and more often—as is the case with estate planning—the documents need to be notarized.

I'm guessing that information must have been on the site somewhere in the fine print—or maybe it was front and center. Regardless, that all-important and vital step for even a lousy set of documents was not taken. Therefore, it was as if no documents had ever been filled out at all.

It is such a good thing that Delia had the sense to make an appointment with my office. I reviewed their DIY documents using my 50-point checklist that I use when I'm evaluating an existing plan. Truth is, I did not even need the checklist—I knew immediately that the DIY documents were doomed to fail. Instead, we created a Revocable Living Trust, documents for incapacity, and a complete Kid Protection Plan®. The latter not only set forth the long-term guardians (in case David and Delia died) but also named short-term guardians for that interim period if David and Delia were merely incapacitated, and we designated people to make medical decisions for the kids in case David and Delia were unable to for whatever reason (death or mere incapacity). Their kids would NEVER wind up in the care of DCFS.

For a fraction of what probate would have cost in their specific situation, we were able to provide them with a comprehensive estate plan that took into account whom they wanted raising their children in the event both of them passed away. I'm happy to say they left my office with peace of mind that their plan would actually work for them if they were merely incapacitated or if they died. Hallelujah!

Chapter 8

Unfunded Uma (You Can't Cross Your T's or Dot Your I's if There Are No Letters)

Are you the kind of person who once a project is done, you never go back and look at it again? Did you create an estate plan 5, 10, or even 15 years ago and have not reviewed it since? Did a "traditional" estate planning attorney put some documents together for you and never bother to follow up to see if there were any changes that occurred that might require an update to your plan? As you read on through this chapter, you'll discover how my office does things differently than a traditional estate planning law office, and you'll understand why I say estate planning is not "one and done."

I have to start the story off by saying even this one blew me away. This is the story of Unfunded Uma.

There are many of these stories that tend to cross over a bit, meaning they encompass several reasons or excuses as to why the person either didn't do an estate plan or why that estate plan will not work. And this one is no exception. As I've indicated in prior chapters (see Chapter 2), if you have real property or minor children, the best way to keep your family out of court and out of conflict—meaning, keeping them out of probate when you die and your estate meets the threshold for probate—is with a comprehensive estate plan.

If you meet even one of those criteria, and you meet your state's requirements—but you don't have an estate plan in place—your assets will have to be run through the probate process to have a judge decide who gets them. Even if you don't have children, siblings, living parents, or other close family members, the court will do what it can to find your heirs (touched on in Chapter 2). If you have no heirs, your assets will be turned over to your state of domicile. When push comes to shove, no one wants that, right? It's kind of like paying taxes—why do it if you can find a legal way not to?

Let's talk about Uma for a moment. She's a single mom by choice. When she came to me, she had an 18-year-old son about to head off to college. They lived in the affluent city of Encino, California.

Prior to finding me, Uma went to a traditional estate planning attorney to get her estate plan done. What do I mean by "traditional" estate attorney? Well . . .

Oh, Traditional . . .

There are many types of attorneys out in the community. There are contract attorneys, personal injury attorneys, bankruptcy attorneys, divorce attorneys (plus many more), and then there are traditional estate planning attorneys. I think it is relatively obvious what contract, personal injury, bankruptcy, and divorce attorneys are. But when it comes to estate planning, there are absolute differences as to how a traditional estate planner approaches planning, and how I—and my colleagues who practice the way I do—approach estate planning.

The traditional estate planning attorney may or may not meet with their prospective clients. I have often heard stories that the initial meeting was with an assistant or maybe a paralegal. Oh sure, the attorney may pop their head into the conference room and say hello to you, but maybe not. The assistant will go ahead and ask a few questions about the prospect's current financial situation, assets, and liabilities—maybe even their income.

They will likely ask about the ages of the children and if the client wants to divide their assets between the children at the client's death.They may explain that a Trust is required to allow their property and assets to pass to their children outside of the court process. An engagement letter will be signed, and a fee charged. The clients will come back a few weeks later and sign documents that the attorney firm prepared.

Ultimately, the clients will receive a lovely binder full of stuff that they have little or no understanding about. The firm may provide a letter of instruction stuck in the binder indicating that all the clients' assets should be moved into the Trust. But, of course, who reads these long, legalese-filled papers? Well . . . I do—but I'm a lawyer!

From my experience, a traditional estate planning attorney is a "one-and-done" document production center. That firm will provide a set of documents, which were prepared with little or no input from the client, and likely no options were discussed. After providing the binder of documents, there will be no ongoing contact from that attorney with those clients. If something in the life of the client changes, or they need additional help and call the lawyer, they will be directed to a secretary, assistant, or paralegal. If the lawyer does get on the phone, a bill for their time will subsequently be sent to the client for that 15-minute phone call. The client may or may not take the steps to ensure that their Trust is "fully funded"—meaning, transferring all of their assets into the Trust, including their family home by way of a new deed.

You see, a Trust is just a document unless and until other steps are taken to actually make sure it will work when it is truly needed. How do I know all this? Well, when my husband and I first got our estate plan prepared many, many years ago (before I started practicing this type of law), our lawyer met with my husband. I was not even there for the first meeting!

Some questions were asked, but nothing was really laid out in terms of choices with explanations as to how each choice might affect things down the line. A set of documents was prepared, which we went into the office to sign. So little was asked of us about what WE wanted to accomplish with that plan. In fact, the lawyer did not even inquire as to whether I was a citizen of the United States. At the time I was solely a Canadian citizen, and without proper planning, that could have resulted in HUGE tax consequences!

Ultimately, we were handed a set of documents in a big binder. It is a good thing that nothing happened to either my husband or to me before I got around to making substantial changes to our estate plan.

We had the "traditional" estate planning experience. We paid a couple thousand dollars for this. Nothing was really tailored to our needs, but rather, whatever the lawyer's software spit out was the plan we got. Fast-forward several years—so much about our lives changed! We acquired new financial accounts, we sold real property, and so on. I became a dual U.S./Canadian citizen. And then the law regarding estate taxes changed. All of those things should have been updated within our Trust documents, but we had no ongoing relationship with that lawyer. So he never even bothered to let us know that our plan would fail.

Now, obviously, I'm a lawyer, and I possess a higher degree of knowledge and understanding about these things . . . especially since I changed over my practice from civil litigation to estate planning. I took a lot of continuing legal education classes so that I could confidently practice in the area of estate planning. Plus, I've gained quite a bit of experience over the last 10+ years working exclusively in this area.

It should also go without saying—but I'll say it anyway! What my office provides is NOT the traditional estate planning attorney experience. It is much, much more. You'll see what I mean shortly.

Back to Uma

When Uma came to me, she was asking about revising her existing Trust documents. You see, they were originally prepared in 2008. At that time, her son was just a little boy. Her financial situation was different. In the interim, she purchased a condominium and a life insurance policy, and she opened a new bank account. No one had reviewed her change in circumstances and advised her on how all of those things affected the efficacy of her Trust. Can you see where this is going?

Prior to coming into my office, Uma filled out my intake forms. By the way, my intake form does, in fact, ask whether the potential client is a citizen of the United States. It also asks for all financial accounts, including bank, brokerage, money market, retirement, and the like—more on this in the next few sentences!

I knew that Uma had a Trust prepared, and I asked that she forward it to me so I could review it ahead of our meeting. When we sat down to discuss everything together, I pulled out the financial spreadsheet I'd created on her behalf. That spreadsheet consisted of all of the accounts that she listed out for me in the intake forms, including the life insurance policy.

The reason I do this is because all of a person's financial assets have to be moved into the Trust in order for them to pass to the beneficiaries of that Trust. If an asset is left out, it could be subject to probate—or worse . . . it could wind up in the state's Department of Unclaimed Property (see Chapter 2) because if it is not claimed, it will wind up with the state.

A traditional estate planning firm does not bother to track your financial assets and may never even mention the possibility that your assets could wind up in the Department of Unclaimed Property. But do you know who does? Me. I do.

In going over Uma's accounts, I asked her if they were all owned by her existing 2008 Trust. She had no idea what I meant. I asked her if the attorney who drafted these documents had provided any instructions about transferring her bank and brokerage accounts into her Trust. They had not.

In fact, none of Uma's accounts had been put into her Trust. Moreover, the condominium she had bought several years before was not in the Trust either. Uma was completely UNFUNDED! Since 2008! Imagine if Uma had died or become incapacitated. That plan she put together in 2008 would have failed.

The kicker in all this? UMA IS A LICENSED ATTORNEY! When she told me she was a lawyer, I think my jaw visibly hit the ground. *WHAT? You are an attorney, and you were unaware that your Trust needed to be funded in order for it to actually do what you wanted it to do?* I'm not implying that every attorney should know this stuff, but learning that even a licensed attorney could be naive to this information—how could any "traditional" estate planning attorney expect laypeople to know?

So, when I tell you that my firm is anything but "traditional"—what I mean is that we provide a full service that contemplates exactly what the client is looking to achieve. We uncover that information because we do the following . . .

a. We obtain some information from the intake forms that are filled out ahead of the initial Family Wealth Planning Session.
b. During that Family Wealth Planning Session, I personally (not my paralegal) meet with the prospective clients and talk with them about their family dynamic, their assets, and their goals regarding passing on their assets to whomever they choose.
c. I discuss and educate what happens when a person does not have a plan and how the probate process works. I explain how a Trust works at various stages of life and death. I go over what estate taxes are, how they've changed over time, and how they could change in the future. We talk about how the Department of Unclaimed Property works and the steps we help them take to ensure they do not lose their own assets. (But you already knew that.)
d. We talk about the different types of documents that are necessary to complete an estate plan and how each one works.
e. We offer choices within the design of the plan regarding passing assets to a spouse (if there is one) and children, with several different options based upon what the client wants to do. It's worth noting that we do not allow our drafting software to dictate the terms.

f. When it comes to funding the Trust, my office takes care of the primary residence transfer, and I walk the client through the steps to transfer every other type of financial account into the Trusts—or how to change designated beneficiaries to ensure the assets pass according to the desires of the client.
g. I assure them that we will meet again in three years to discuss their plan and to see if any changes need to be made because of a change in circumstances or changes in the law. But if they need me before three years, they are invited to call. And no, there will not be a bill sent after any phone call.
h. There is more, but I think you get the picture.

Phew!

Uma got lucky. She came to me and began to understand how her estate plan would have failed if she had died without properly funding her Trust. Moreover—here is that crossover I mentioned at the beginning—her 18-year-old son who was heading off to college also needed documents in case he became incapacitated. She hadn't even thought about this!

Remember, once your child turns 18 (in most states), they are deemed to be legal adults, and legal authority is required to act on their behalf. This usually comes in the form of legal documents such as a power of attorney for finances and a healthcare directive for medical decisions (see Chapter 15 for more details).

We were not only able to restate Uma's Trust, but we walked her through how to become fully FUNDED! In addition, we prepared a set of documents to ensure that Uma was legally permitted to act on her son's behalf in the event of his incapacity. Take that to college!

Chapter 9

Prepared Patty and Prodigal Pete (What's Yours Is Yours)

Are you and your spouse yin and yang? Did you find that when it comes to your mate, opposites attract? Is one of you the CFO (chief financial officer) of the family and the other the COS (chief officer of spending)? Have you had conversations with your significant other about how money should be spent or saved? The avatars in this story could not be more different in their approach to money. Here, I will show you how multiple solutions exist within the estate planning arena for even these types of contrasting views.

Yes, the Sheila and Arnie story of Chapter 1 was relatively arduous for all three of us because there was a lot of emotion wrapped up in conversations about money and expectations. But having those kinds of hard conversations is a necessary part of life, not just in terms of your estate plan.

I'm not telling you something you don't already know. Having these hard conversations can be trying, but that doesn't mean people can't come to an agreement and find common ground. The path to getting there can be stressful. Part of my job is to help ease that stress and to help the family get to a resolution.

Some clients come to me full of indecision. They know they need to create a plan, but there are so many factors that they are concerned about, and they're unsure about how to deal with it all. The future is unknown, except for the fact that we are all going to die. And from that perspective alone, isn't it better to prepare your family for what you know is coming someday?

Think back to when you were in school. You knew you had that test coming for your least favorite class (fill in the blank). Maybe you didn't like math so much, but you knew you could get through it if you were prepared. So, what did you do? Ideally, you made a plan to gather your class notes, review your homework, and do some practice questions. These steps were taken so that you could walk into the testing room knowing that you had done all that you could do in order to perform the best that you could on that test.

There are a lot of similarities with estate planning. Clients need to be prepared to make decisions and committed to getting it done.

I've said it before and I'll say it again—we're all going to die, and it's better to do so with a plan in place. It's better for your peace of mind, better for your family, and better for the transition between living and dying.

Keep in mind that simply because you have some of those hard conversations, it doesn't mean that things are all finished. There is more to it than that. And this next story is one that involves not only potentially uncomfortable conversations—but also clients confronting a potentially emotionally charged issue that can really put the family at odds if not handled delicately.

Before we get started, I need to interject that unless you are in a registered domestic partnership, the law observes two people living together as strangers, and the creation of a joint Trust becomes far more complicated. In my office, it is not recommended. That aside, this chapter is focused on married couples. This next situation was an interesting scenario, and anyone in a committed relationship will probably relate.

Everyone comes into a marriage with their own relationship to money (of course their own baggage too). Some good and healthy, and some not so much. Let's say you are the spouse who is good with money—such as budgeting and controlled spending—but what happens if your partner is a borderline spendthrift? What if your partner spends almost every dollar they earn when left to their own devices? This can present a substantial concern for both parties to the equation. And so begins the story of Prepared Patty and her husband, Prodigal Pete.

Rainy-Day-er Versus Big Spender

Patty and Pete were a married couple in their early 40s with three kids ranging in age from six to ten. They owned a home and had fairly typical financial assets, including life insurance, retirement accounts, certificates of deposit, and a small savings account. Patty was one of those folks who like to be as prepared as possible for every conceivable scenario.

In reviewing her intake forms, I noticed that she answered every question and also came to the office with an accordion folder—bank statements, life insurance policies, the deed to their home, retirement account statements, and even a list of five or six charitable organizations to whom she wanted to leave cash gifts! I mean, this woman had it all together and then some! (Love her!)

Mind you, I do not ask my clients to provide me with these documents unless there is some definitive reason for me to see them. Occasionally, I do need to review documents, but generally not bank statements and the like. Nevertheless, she brought them. Prepared Patty was ready and committed to the process.

Pete, on the other hand, really had not given much thought to the questions presented on the intake forms. He was along for the ride, as is typical with some husbands who allow their wives to take the laboring oar in these matters.

When we all sat down together and started the conversations, I could sense that Patty was a bit on edge. So, I asked what was on her mind. With Pete sitting right there in the room, Patty relayed to me that she came into the office prepared but also apprehensive and rather fearful. I urged her to tell me more.

Patty explained that her ailing father was a very wealthy man. She and her sibling each expected to inherit multiple millions when Dad eventually passed away. Of course, at that point, I was thinking to myself that this is the kind of problem many of us would not mind taking on . . .

But why was Patty so fearful? I knew there had to be more to the story. Patty described herself as a saver. She believed in rainy-day funds. She loved to vacation but had learned to do so on a strict budget. With three growing (and often hungry) kids, there were a lot of household expenses, including kid activities, school supplies, clothing, braces, and medical care, to name a few.

Patty was the one who made sure the bills were all paid. She was the family CFO—even though Pete earned the majority of their combined income. Pete on the other hand, as Patty described him, was "a big spender."

They had grown up in very different realms. Patty's family had money but was not cavalier in spending it. They had what they needed and some "extras" but did not live an extravagant lifestyle. Patty did not want for anything while growing up, but she was taught about money, how to use it, and how not to waste it. These values were passed down to Patty by her parents, and she embraced them.

Pete grew up in a much different set of circumstances. His parents split early in his life, and his mother dealt with mental health issues and drug addiction. He and his sister (who had passed away by the time he came to my office) often had to "figure out" how to take care of themselves. There was never enough money in his household when he was young. As a result of this, once Pete got his college degree and started making money, he either consciously or unconsciously began spending what he earned on anything he wanted—whether that be fine food and drink, adult-sized toys (he had quite the sports car . . .), sporting goods, concert tickets, you name it.

Pete was of the mindset that as an adult, he was not going to be deprived like he had been growing up. Talking about all of this brought up a lot of untapped emotion for Pete. I have to say, I definitely understood this point of view.

Patty's fear was that if she were the first to pass away, she believed her spendthrift spouse would blow right through all that inheritance money, leaving virtually nothing for their three kids. Naturally, Pete denied it would ever happen, but Patty did not back down. She provided examples that I do not need to relay here. Suffice it to say, Pete was certainly capable of spending a lot of money if given the opportunity.

Understandable Caution

Are you in a similar circumstance, where your spouse is not a planner, saver, or budgeter, and you know you will have a substantial inheritance coming to you? Does this weigh heavily on your mind? What if you will not be inheriting millions from your family but a more modest amount? Are you concerned that any amount you may receive from your family could disappear at the hands of your spouse? Do you fear that if you are the first to die, your *spousey* might spend it all before the kids even get to college and leave nothing for them?

I really love estate planning because—almost no matter what issues the clients present with—there are legitimate and legal tools and solutions to deal with most if not all of those issues through a well-drafted estate plan. Patty and Pete were no exception! There are absolutely multiple ways to handle this scenario.

For those of you who reside in California, you need to be aware that we are a Community Property State. Unless a couple has a prenuptial agreement in place, just about everything they acquire after marriage is considered a community asset. EXCEPT . . . inheritance.

When one receives an inheritance from a family member—such as a parent—that inheritance is NOT considered a community asset. While there are a few other instances where after-acquired property is not deemed part of the community, those are not relevant here. The receiving spouse would have to take actual, specific steps with the intention of making the inheritance a community asset in order for their spouse to be able to consider and treat it as though it were a community asset. This is an important factor in the story of Patty and Pete.

Oh, Great Relief!

I educated Patty about these facts. She needed to understand that if she wanted to keep the millions of dollars she was going to inherit from her father as a separate asset—one that Pete could not access, even after Patty's death—we could absolutely plan for that. In fact, there are various mechanisms within the estate planning toolbox that allow for this precise situation.

We discussed several alternative courses of action. We specifically discussed one where, even after death, Patty would be in control of whether Pete could access any of the funds. As another potential plan, Patty could set up her own separate Trust purely consisting of the inherited assets, with an independent Successor Trustee (not Pete). This would make her children the beneficiaries when they attained certain ages.

Another plan was to create a joint Trust that would split into separate Trusts at the death of the first spouse. In that scenario, Patty's separate assets would be held for the benefit of her children, not for Pete. Or Patty could allow Pete SOME access but not complete access.

So many options!

Needless to say, Patty felt a great sense of relief knowing that Pete would not have carte blanche with her dad's money. In the end, we formed a plan in the event that Patty would be the first to die. Pete would get some access to help support his living expenses while raising the children. But he would not be given a blank check.

Pete acknowledged that Patty's inheritance was hers to do what she wanted with. He also appreciated the fact that Patty wanted to take care of him and the children if Patty were the first to die. It was a beautiful thing to see.

Chapter 10

Overconfident Omar (Knowing It All Doesn't Mean You Get It Right)

Are you the person in the room who has the solution to every problem? Do you believe your way is always the right way? If so, you might want to skip this chapter! Here, we will explore how things can go awry if you rely on non-estate-planning documents to transfer your assets at the time of your death, and how your family might be left high and dry unless you plan appropriately while you are still alive.

Ick, I am not thrilled with this story because of the frustration it evokes within me. Maybe you can relate? I think every one of us knows someone who has the mentality that they're just smarter than everyone else in the room. You know the type . . . they believe they are the expert on everything. It does not matter what the subject is or what the issue might be; they have all the answers. You can't tell them anything. So annoying, amiright? I mean, I hope this isn't you—but if it is, you probably should just skip this chapter.

This leads me right to the story of Overconfident Omar.

A few years back, a couple came to my office to talk about estate planning. Omar and Olivia had two young children. They lived in an affluent neighborhood near the area of my office, and Olivia and I sort of knew each other because we have mutual friends. She contacted me about getting their estate plan together—and of course, I was happy to help.

They scheduled time with me. And let me take a moment to comment here . . . I generally set aside about 60–90 minutes *prior to the meeting* to go over the intake forms that I ask everyone to complete. This is my time; I do not charge clients for it. I take it upon myself to try to know something about the clients before they come into the office. Those intake forms ask a lot of questions, including the location, type, and amount of assets in each of the financial accounts the couple has. I do not ask for this information because I'm trying to be nosy—I ask for it because this information is relevant to many different aspects of the estate plan, including the following . . .

- Whether there are designated beneficiaries (on life insurance and retirement accounts)
- Whether there might be an estate tax issue to discuss (this varies from state to state, but the Federal Estate Tax exemption is something I discuss with all clients)

And this information also allows me to calculate what the approximate cost of probate might be for the family if no plan is put in place. Moreover, the intake forms ask about the goals clients have for planning, and even asks questions such as

"What is the most important thing to make sure we talk about together?" I do not assign my assistant or anyone else to go over these completed intake forms. I do it myself.

When I sat down with Omar and Olivia's intake forms, I was actually surprised. From what they submitted ahead of the meeting, it was pretty clear that Omar was having no part of that process. He and Olivia provided their home address, and that was it. Not one bank account, brokerage account, life insurance policy, or retirement account was listed—not even the financial institutions where such accounts might be housed.

They did list a couple of people they had thought about for potential guardians for their children—but otherwise the forms were blank. As I sat staring at the lack of information for me to assimilate, I thought to myself, *Hmmm, this planning session is going to be a challenge.* Well, at least that freed up an extra hour for me that day!

What Do You Tell the Person Who Knows Everything?

Just before the meeting, I tried to prepare myself for pushback. Somehow, after all the years I have been in practice, I just kind of have a sense for how it might go. I wasn't wrong.

I have a specific process that I go through with just about every new client. What I like to do is to start with a written agenda that is sitting on the conference room table when new clients come in. I always introduce myself and then walk through the agenda so that the potential clients have an idea of what to expect. With Omar and Olivia, I launched into a discussion about my firm, how I got to this place, a bit about me personally, and then I asked the clients to talk to me about themselves.

As with all of my clients, I was interested to know their family dynamic (were their parents still alive, do they have siblings, are they a close family, was anyone on the outs, etc.). I also wanted to know how they met and about their career backgrounds. In addition, I love to see pictures of their young kids!

One of the few great things about the changing world of COVID, when most of my meetings were held via Zoom, was that I often got to actually see the kids on camera! Otherwise, I almost never get to meet the kids, but I like to see pictures because, after all, our kids are our most important asset!

My intention is to build a foundation of trust while getting to know more about them. Next, I asked what brought them to me and what, if any, experience they had with family members passing away with or without plans in place. Omar was having none of that. Right from the start, Omar tried to control the meeting.

After I walked through the first part of my agenda, talked about myself, my practice, my family—as I always do—I asked them if they had any questions about what I had said, or perhaps what I hadn't said. Now, I can say with assurance that most clients appreciate my openness and thank me for sharing my story. Occasionally, they will ask a question, particularly about the ongoing relationship that I maintain with my clients (my policy is to meet with clients every three years at no additional charge to review their plans with them, because life happens and sometimes changes are needed, or the law could change, which might affect their plan).

And then, there's Omar. The guy who knows exactly how he can "end-around" estate planning. HA!

Omar started asking all kinds of questions that had nothing to do with me, my process, or anything that I had discussed with him. He wanted to know why his family even needed a Trust . . . How would a Trust be better than a transfer on death deed? How would a Trust operate for pay-on-death accounts? What was wrong with using a beneficiary designation? What was wrong with a statutory power of attorney and healthcare directive? Why couldn't he just tell his twin brother what he wanted to have done with his assets and let the brother handle things?

Oh, and what was I planning to charge him to put in place all of these things he could accomplish without doing an estate plan? Obviously, Omar had spent some time on Google and picked up a few terms.

Rather than try to go through the many problems with each of the concepts Omar raised, I simply told him that I would be happy to explain why creating an estate plan with an attorney was a better approach. But before I went there, I already knew there was no response that I could provide to Omar that would satisfy his firmly held belief that he didn't need me or anyone else to tell him how to protect his family and assets. He was set on the idea that his twin brother was perfectly capable of fulfilling Omar's wishes without having to do some "expensive" Trust document. At that point in the meeting, the amount of fees for the plan hadn't even come up!

Nevertheless, I decided to try. (Can't blame a girl for trying!) I told Omar that my intention was to talk about each of the questions he had asked after I gathered more information about him and Olivia, but that I could tell he wanted answers before he would commit to opening that door. So, I explained that if he left the funds outright to his brother via a transfer or pay on death, the brother could do anything he wanted with those assets—including losing them in a divorce, to a creditor, or in a lawsuit.

Omar would have no control over what happens to those assets once he passes away. And while it's possible that the brother would separate his own assets from Omar's, it would be complicated, expensive, and risky. There was also a huge risk that a pay-on-death proceeds would never make it to Omar's children. If the twin brother passed away, Omar's kids would be completely left out of the inheritance of Omar's (former) assets. The assets would pass to the twin brother's kids. Seriously.

It was no surprise that Overconfident Omar stood on his belief that he could handle all of his assets via either a transfer on death or a pay on death for each account (whatever those might have been) that he had. It really didn't matter what I said at that moment.

At the end of the day, I told Omar that I was not trying to sell him something. And if he did not see the value in the services I provide, he was welcome to handle things in any way he saw fit. And there's the thing . . . I could have offered the plan to Omar for free, and he still would have believed his way of doing things was the better way.

This next section is just between you and me: we will leave Omar out of this . . .

Avoidable Pitfalls

A Transfer on Death (TOD) is a legal arrangement that allows you to transfer your assets to your named beneficiaries after your death without the need for probate. On the other hand, a Revocable Living Trust (RLT) also allows you to transfer your assets to your named beneficiaries without the need for probate, but it provides more flexibility during your lifetime.

There are many potential pitfalls of using a TOD instead of a RLT, and here are just a few:

> **Limited flexibility:** A TOD account or deed can only be changed or revoked by the account or deed owner, making it a rigid and inflexible arrangement. On the other hand, a Trust can be changed or revoked by the Trust creator at any time, providing more flexibility during their lifetime.

No protection against incapacity: A TOD does not offer any protection against incapacity or disability since the transfer of assets only takes place upon the owner's death. In contrast, an RLT can provide for incapacity planning by naming a Successor Trustee who can manage the Trust assets in case the Trust creator becomes incapacitated.

No privacy protection: Since a TOD transfer happens outside of probate, it becomes a matter of public record, which means anyone can access the information about the transfer. In contrast, an RLT transfer happens privately and does not become a matter of public record.

No asset management: A TOD account or deed transfer does not provide any asset management or protection for the beneficiaries. In contrast, an RLT can provide for ongoing management and protection of the Trust assets for the benefit of the named beneficiaries.

No asset protection: A TOD transfer does not provide any asset protection to the beneficiaries. In contrast, an RLT can provide asset protection to the Trust assets from the creditors of the beneficiaries.

And finally, ZERO control: A TOD transfer takes your asset and gives it to someone else without instruction or limitation. If you leave everything to your twin brother in hopes that he will take care of your family, he is under no legal obligation to do so. (Moral obligation is a whole different category.)

As you can likely see, even though Omar cannot, estate planning isn't just about handing over your assets for someone else to control. It is about setting forth your wishes to take care of your family in the manner you see fit. Maybe Omar's brother is a stand-up guy who would do the right thing—but why would anyone ever take that chance?

Please know that there is an easy, effective, legal, affordable, and secure way to carry out your desires to protect your assets and your family. I am CONFIDENT you get what I mean. And if not, I wish you well with your decisions. All the best!

Chapter 11

Superstitious Sally (Will Death Take a Holiday?)

Are you apprehensive to talk about death? Do you fear it to the point where you cannot even have a conversation about dying or incapacity? For some, this is a cultural phenomenon, and for others it might be generational. This chapter looks at how one family suffered because their matriarch refused to think about death, let alone get a plan in place to deal with the inevitable.

Sally was a 65-year-old woman who grew up in a traditional Asian family. In her culture, talking about death was seen as a bad omen and was avoided at all costs. Sally had always felt uneasy about the topic and had never discussed it with anyone, not even her family members. Despite her age, and perhaps even her underlying understanding that she needed to do something about her end-of-life care and distribution of her assets—she did nothing.

The thought of discussing the end of her life gripped her with fear. Those old, traditional values that had been instilled in her precluded her from allowing herself to even think about "planning" for her death—let alone talk about it with friends, family, or a lawyer. When her adult children brought up the topic of creating an estate plan, Sally became visibly uncomfortable and refused to talk about it. She believed that talking about death would bring her own demise and that it was better to avoid the topic altogether. She would either walk away or wave her hand to dismiss the conversation.

Sally's adult children (clients of mine) were concerned about their mother's well-being. They tried to reason with her and explain the importance of creating an estate plan. They reached out to me to see if I could help. However, this was one of those situations where there was nothing I could do to show Sally that her concerns were misplaced . . .

The Worst-Case Scenario

Are you still planning on living forever? Are you still thinking like an immortal teenager or twenty-something-year-old? I hope not . . .

Clearly, we will all pass away at some point. And talking about this unfortunate fact and establishing a plan for it does not invite an early death. Death and dying have remained somewhat taboo subjects despite our guaranteed mortality. Many people are afraid of dying, but Sally took it to a substantially different level. I do not believe Sally's situation is the norm—nevertheless, there are a percentage of people who share her strong beliefs.

Imagine asking any scientist, physician, psychologist, or sociologist if discussing death or planning around it brings it about. I am certain the response would be a collective "No." In fact, I have been practicing estate planning for years, and there has not been one incident where an otherwise healthy client of mine suddenly died within days, weeks, or even months of creating that estate plan.

Is there any way to make that point to someone who, to their innermost core, believes that speaking of such things causes them to happen? Well, Sally remained firm in her belief that talking about this topic would bring about the end and her own mortality. She refused to discuss it or make any plans, and she never agreed to meet with me.

No, Death Won't Happen to You ;)

Unfortunately, the worst-case scenario happened. I was contacted by the family about a year after they asked me to speak to her. Sally suffered a sudden heart attack and was rushed to the hospital. She did not recover and passed away without any end-of-life plans such as the following . . .

- Making her wishes known about cremation or burial
- Establishing how she wanted to pass on her assets
- Instructing family as to how her outstanding creditors should be paid
- Identifying which family member would handle her existing estate

Her adult children were left to speculate what Sally would have wanted: burial or cremation? Funeral or celebration of life? A small gathering or a large church event?

Both adult siblings had a difference of opinion on these and other issues that arose after Sally passed away. Moreover, her family was left to navigate the complicated and stressful process of probate, which was made more difficult by their mother's reluctance to discuss any aspect of her final wishes.

Would she have wanted certain family heirlooms to be divided between the adult children—or some to go to Sally's other family members? What about her real estate? One of her adult children had been living in the home helping to take care of her. Unfortunately, there were not enough liquid assets to pay out half the value of the property to the other sibling, so that adult child was going to have to move out. This caused significant conflict between the siblings.

Neglect or Superstition?

Sally's situation illustrates the fear and reluctance that some individuals may have when it comes to discussing death and creating an estate plan due to cultural superstition. It is not completely uncommon for people to have fears due to cultural and generational superstitions, which in turn present challenges when attempting to talk about death. In many cultures, death is viewed as a prohibited topic, and discussing it openly may be considered disrespectful or unlucky. However, it is important to recognize that avoiding the topic of death and neglecting to create an estate plan can have serious consequences for the individual's loved ones. Additionally, important end-of-life decisions, such as medical care and funeral arrangements, may be left up to chance.

If someone is hesitant to create an estate plan due to fear or superstition, I would certainly try to approach the topic with empathy and understanding. I acknowledge that discussing death can be difficult and uncomfortable. But simultaneously, I cannot emphasize enough the importance of creating a plan to ensure that desires are respected and loved ones are taken care of. This is the whole point of creating an estate plan—ensuring your loved ones are not left with a big mess to clean up. That conflict that so often ensues among family members is forestalled because you make all of the decisions about what should happen while you are alive.

Ultimately, it is important to respect an individual's beliefs and work with them to find a solution that aligns with their values and goals. However, it is also important to try to impart upon the reluctant planner the potential consequences of neglecting to create an estate plan and encourage the individual to take steps to protect their assets and their loved ones.

Perhaps that means enlisting the help of a spiritual leader from their culture or enlisting the services of a death doula. I am still scratching my head over this one. But I encourage you to keep trying if this is your situation. It's better for everyone to have a hard conversation than to be left scratching your own heads as to what needs to happen when the inevitable arrives.

Chapter 12

Cheap Charlie (A Penny Saved by Not Estate Planning Is a Million Pennies Gifted to the State)

Have you heard of those old sayings "penny-wise and pound-foolish" and "you get what you pay for"? Or are you intimately familiar with the value of items at the 99¢ Store? There are certain services that—if pursuing the cheapest available—will not provide the necessary protections you likely want for your family and loved ones. Such is the case with estate planning. Here, our avatar puts himself and his family at great risk because cost was the most important factor in his mind.

In my opinion, there are some things you simply do not do on the cheap, and since I'm the one writing this book, I am going to share some of my thoughts in this regard:

1. **Health care:** Investing in quality health care is essential to ensure long-term physical and mental well-being. Opting for cheap health care options may save money in the short term, but it can lead to serious health consequences in the long run. I have a story about this in my own family—but I think that one might be an entire book unto itself. Suffice to say, I've personally learned this lesson.

2. **Safety equipment:** When it comes to personal safety, it is crucial not to cut corners. This includes purchasing reliable and durable safety equipment such as helmets, seat belts, fire extinguishers, and smoke detectors. When you really sit down and think about the safety of yourself and your own person, you may be willing to compromise. But when you conjure up an image of your family and how best to protect them, I'd bet my house that you think twice about cheaping out on these types of safeguards!

3. **Home repairs:** Home repairs are an essential aspect of maintaining a healthy living environment. Attempting to cut costs by opting for cheap repairs or DIY solutions can lead to shoddy workmanship and potentially dangerous living conditions. I refer you back to exhibit A—if you recall, I mentioned my husband's attempt to repair the kitchen sink in Chapter 7, which resulted in two days at my house with no running water! And guess what? We hired a plumber who was able to rectify the

problem in just over an hour. I commend my husband for his efforts, but some things you just need to leave to the professionals!

4. **Education:** Education is a lifelong investment in personal and professional growth. Opting for cheap or low-quality educational programs may save money in the short term, but it can limit career opportunities and hinder personal growth in the long run. And think about it—do you want the guy who did an online, self-taught program to be fixing the brakes on your car? Or do you want to entrust your vehicle to the fully certified auto mechanic who proudly displays their diploma and certification of completion for the world to see?

But most of all . . .

5. **Legal help:** When it comes to legal matters, it is essential to seek advice from a qualified and experienced lawyer. Opting for cheap legal services or attempting to handle legal issues independently can lead to costly mistakes and negative long-term consequences.

Of course, I have a clear bias in this regard, but #5 is a real thing—and this leads me into the story of Cheap Charlie . . .

Cost and Volume

Charlie and his wife, Colleen, were referred to me by a mutual friend who also happened to be a lawyer. They're not an estate planning lawyer, mind you, but rather an insurance defense attorney who worked in a large downtown Los Angeles law firm. Now, I did not prepare the estate plan for this attorney, nor had he ever even discussed with me how my process works or the fees I charge for the services I provide. Nevertheless, unknown to me, this attorney "friend" who referred Charlie to me had given Charlie his two cents opinion as to what an estate plan should cost. Needless to say, Charlie came to my office with a preconceived notion that my Cadillac service would come at a Cracker Jack price (or for those who don't attend baseball games, a luxury item at a fast-food price).

Charlie and Colleen were very nice people who had one young child. They owned a house in a beach city and had additional assets. The unique thing about this couple is that neither of them is a United States citizen. From an estate planning perspective, this adds a layer that MUST be addressed so that the estate is not considered "foreign" under the law by the IRS. I mentioned in Chapter 8 that when my husband and I did our initial planning way back when, the attorney failed to ask about our citizenship. This is critical because the tax structure difference for a U.S. citizen versus a noncitizen is extreme.

There is a tax provision that allows for married couples who are United States citizens to transfer an *unlimited amount of assets to each other* during their lifetimes or at death without incurring any federal estate or gift tax per year. However, the non-US Spouse can only receive *$175,000 per year* in gifts from the US citizen spouse as of 2023. (Please note: this figure is indexed for inflation, and thus will be different depending on the year.) What a huge difference! If not dealt with properly, Charlie's and Colleen's estates (the stuff, money, and property they own at death) could be facing a massive tax bill at their respective deaths.

Herein lies a real difference between working with a low-cost, high-volume law firm as compared to a qualified and knowledgeable estate planning attorney—who takes time to speak to their potential clients about issues that can substantially impact their estate plan. There are ways of handling this exact situation with various planning techniques to adjust for residency and citizenship. A lawyer offering estate planning services and Trusts for $2,000 or less is likely with a big volume, minimal service firm more concerned with the number of clients they are bringing in every month than providing you with a quality plan that will actually work when you need it.

Penny-Wise, Many Pounds Foolish

Getting back to Charlie and his preconceived notions of cost... after getting to know one another, Colleen, Charlie, and I went through the education portion of my initial planning session. We determined that they had a real need for not only planning for their minor child, but also planning for the fact that neither was a United States citizen. I presented my plan options, including what services were provided and the cost under each package. My clients choose their own fee based upon the options that are most important and relevant to their family's needs. I lay those options out prior to the design of their plan. I am not a one-size-fits-all, bargain basement, bulk plan firm.

It was clear from the look on Charlie's face that he was sticker-shocked. At that point, I checked in with him to try to get an understanding of what he was thinking. It was at that moment he mentioned our mutual attorney "friend" had quoted a price substantially lower than the packages I presented.

As a side note, I want to say that I'm fairly certain the mutual attorney friend meant no harm in quoting a fee to Charlie. He just did so without even a scrap of information to support the "guesstimate" he provided to Charlie. Personally, I would never undertake to provide anyone with an amount another lawyer might charge for their services. Every aspect of the industry is different. Some attorneys charge by the hour—those who have been in practice longer will charge a higher hourly rate. Some attorneys work on flat fees or take a retainer. There are so many variations!

Maybe you've heard that before investing in a professional service you should get three estimates. While often this is wise advice—especially when it comes to car repairs and home remodel projects—it's actually a bad idea when it comes to estate planning. However, you can ensure you get the most efficient and affordable plan possible for your family without shopping for estate planning lawyers.

Let me walk you through why getting three estimates for an estate plan doesn't work to actually get you what you want . . .

Big Shopping Problems

First and foremost, this recommendation assumes that you should be "shopping" for an estate plan based on the ***lowest cost***. It also assumes that you understand exactly what you are shopping for and how to evaluate those estimates! While cost might be *one* factor to consider, it really helps to know what it is that you are slated to receive for the money paid—not to mention knowing what your goals for your estate plan are when you walk in the door.

Moreover, once you hear the cost, how are you going to make a determination that what you are paying for actually meets your objectives and expectations? Herein lies one of the biggest problems with "shopping" with a price in the forefront of your mind. Most people do not truly understand what it means to create an estate plan and what it can do for them. Instead, they are just thinking, *How much does it cost?*

Unfortunately, we see the negative effects of cheap estate planning when family members come to us during a time of grief—with that fancy binder that sat on the shelf for years—sending out signals of false security. With out-of-date estate planning documents, they find themselves stuck in court or conflict—even though that's exactly what their loved one thought they had paid someone to handle!

"Shopping" for an estate plan based on getting the lowest-cost plan possible is the fastest path to leaving your family with an empty set of documents. Maybe those pages are in a beautiful binder, but they're not worth the paper they are written on—and they won't actually work for your family when they need it.

Here are five reasons shopping for the cheapest estate plan is likely to leave you with a plan that won't work for your family . . .

1. The least expensive plan isn't worth the paper it's written on once you've left the attorney's office. Your life changes, the law changes, and your assets change over time—your plan needs to keep up with those changes. And the truth of the matter is that a lawyer can't afford to provide anything more than documents that won't get updated when you only pay a few hundred dollars or even a couple of thousand dollars for a plan. The business model simply doesn't work. It is about the volume of clients, not the service to those clients.

2. Cheap estate plans are often sold by financial professionals who want to get their hands on your money, not do right by your family. Cheap plans are not often sold by an attorney who has built a practice to actually serve your family's best interests. The latter cannot make a living selling $1,000 or even $2,000 plans. Only insurance and financial professionals who get paid commissions to sell annuities and life insurance products to your family (whether they need them or not) can make a living selling cheap documents. Buyer beware!

3. Forms and documents won't be there for your family when you can't be. You want to leave your loved ones in a relationship with a trusted advisor with whom YOU have built a relationship based on trust during your lifetime.
4. You get what you pay for. Unfortunately, your family pays the price when you use a traditional "forms and documents" firm that creates documents without ensuring assets were owned in the right way—or that the plan stays up to date over time. You might think that's malpractice, but it's not. It's common practice, and it leaves your family at risk if/when something happens to you!
5. An estate plan isn't a set-it-and-forget-it kind of thing. It needs to stay up to date with changes in your life, the law, and your assets. Buying a new property, opening a new investment account, having another child, or receiving substantial inheritance can change your tax bracket!

Proceed with Love

If what you want is the false security of a cheap estate plan—like it appeared Charlie wanted—keep on shopping. Chances are you haven't done that because you know that it is risky business, and you treasure your family too much for that. You love your family; I know you do. That's why you picked up this book. You know you want a plan that will work for the people you love when they need it.

Charlie and Colleen walked out of my office without having created an estate plan. It seemed that I was unable to overcome the idea implanted in their minds that cost was the most important factor to consider when establishing an estate plan. I have no idea if they went on to find another attorney or not. However, what I did was send them a letter reminding them that, during our Family Wealth Planning Session, we established (1) they needed the services discussed and (2) the most important thing to them was the safety and care of their child—particularly given that they had no family in this country.

In addition, I outlined some of the specific questions they should ask the next lawyer they interviewed for an estate plan. Now, I know that most estate planning firms simply do not cover the aspects that I do when creating an estate plan. But hey, when you are cheap like Charlie, the only thing to consider is how much it costs. Sorry, Charlie!

Chapter 13

Adolescent Ava and Complete Cherise (You're Never Too Young for Estate Planning)

Do you feel that you are too young to think about the matters in this book? Have you found great success in your endeavors but are now realizing there is more to money than simply making or spending it? Are you prepared for the worst-case scenario of unexpectedly leaving permanently or temporarily? Just because you're under 30 does not mean you don't need a plan.

At age 21 and under, chances are though, you would not meet the criteria for probate, including having your own children, owning assets that exceed the probate threshold, or owning real property. Given these facts, a young adult likely does not need a Revocable Living Trust. However, what about at ages 22–25? At that point, you may have graduated college and begun finding your long-term job/career and investing in your employer-sponsored 401(k). So, is that an appropriate time?

It's really interesting because today things are much different from when I was growing up. We did not have the internet yet, and as we all know, the internet has opened up a whole new world of information and opportunities to the younger generations. These days, a young adult (and even children for that matter) can become an "influencer" and actually make money with the internet. For example, they can post videos showing others how to apply makeup, write in a journal, dance, or play video games. They might start a modeling, music, or an acting career by posting videos on YouTube or TikTok. Really, the possibilities are endless. There are so many ways for the younger generation to create wealth and earn money that most people never even thought of back in my day.

Further, I find that young adults have a lot of courage and creativity and even start their own businesses. From this perspective, let's take a look at Adolescent Ava.

Oh, Ava. She has a complicated and somewhat tragic story. At 25 years old, she already had a thriving farmers' market business. Her boyfriend's mom and Ava had started it when she was 23. Very much interested in nature and growing her own sustainable food, Ava was able to create a wonderful internet sales business, selling her specialty farm fresh goods during the week. On weekends, they would bring the whole operation to the local farmers' market, where they had direct-to-consumer sales. Even though Ava had accumulated some debt, her business was good! Ava was reinvesting in her business, making some inroads in paying off both personal and business debt, as well as setting aside some savings.

But then, a truly unfortunate thing happened. All Ava remembers is that there was a major accident. She was driving. She woke up in jail. And it wasn't until later that she was informed that a friend of hers was dead. Suddenly, Ava found herself in a heap of legal trouble. The situation required her to hire attorneys. On top of potential criminal charges, Ava was being sued by her deceased friend's family for hundreds of thousands of dollars that she did not have. She was concerned about protecting the assets that she did have, including the business interests she shared with her boyfriend's mother. She also had an enormous amount of guilt over the death of her friend, but Ava knew she did not have the kind of money the family wanted to extract from her upon the death of their child. It was all very confusing, sad, and complex. Ava knew she was in trouble and needed significant legal guidance.

Ava was referred to me by another very good friend of hers.

The Referral

Cherise, 26 years old, was also someone who made her living via the internet, as an internet "influencer." While I'm not 100 percent sure of what that means, I know that whatever she was doing, Cherise had made herself a nice sum of money, which was evident when she'd filled out my intake forms a year earlier when she had come to me for estate planning.

She didn't have much in the way of family—a brother and a much-loved dog. But she had a whole host of friends whom she trusted and that she was close to. I was amazed when she came to me to get her estate plan put together. Cherise was by far the youngest client I had ever seen in my estate planning practice.

The reason Cherise came to me was because she had seen firsthand how nasty probate could be when her grandmother passed away. Her grandmother's estate had taken years to resolve through the probate court. There were multiple lawyers, hearings, battles, and fights among Cherise's family. Over what? Money, property, and material items that everyone wanted to stake a claim to. Cherise had lived with her grandmother and taken care of her the last few years of her grandmother's life. Cherise was not very familiar with estate planning at the time (at 20-something years old, who could blame her?), but she knew her grandmother had an older Will. When her grandmother started to have issues with dementia, Cherise was concerned it was too late to update the Will.

Cherise was right. Generally, when a person begins to show signs of dementia, an estate planning lawyer can create or update an estate plan, as long as the attorney can legitimately determine capacity in the moment that the update is discussed, and then again when the updates are signed. The American Bar Association has a checklist for a lawyer to follow, with specific questions to ask for the lawyer to make that determination. Those questions are asked during the design updates and again at the time of signing. Any notary involved can also refuse to acknowledge signatures if they believe capacity is in question.

Obviously, there are risks inherent with making the capacity determination. Often, lawyers will seek outside counsel to interview the client with potential diminished capacity in order to remove any bias in the determination. However, in Cherise's situation, her grandmother's circumstances did not lend themselves to updating her Will. As a result, Cherise and her family went to court to fight out the validity of Grandma's Will and who was to get which assets Grandma owned at her death.

This court battle drove Cherise's family apart, and at the end of it all, Cherise was fairly sure that her grandmother's wishes were not fully honored. Cherise told me she never wanted to have to put her family or friends through that type of horrible court experience. And that is how she found me.

We put together a beautiful plan for Cherise, including provisions to ensure that her beloved dog would never wind up at a shelter and would have sufficient funds to take care of him from Cherise's estate. She was able to designate her brother and trusted friends in all of the fiduciary roles. Further, Cherise made provisions that the family members from whom she was estranged would not be able to make a claim for her assets when she passed away. I am so very proud of Cherise for taking these important steps to get her plan in place at such a young age. Cherise's plan was happily complete.

No Hiding Allowed

In direct contrast, Ava had gone down a path of irresponsible adolescent behavior. Granted, she did not intend the consequences of her actions, but they happened nonetheless, and someone died. It was a really hard pill to swallow, but Ava took ownership of her actions and knew she would face some pretty tough times ahead. Adolescent Ava felt very remorseful.

She came to me with a series of questions regarding how she could protect what little she had left. Of course, I informed Ava that we could not "hide" her assets, because that could be considered fraud by the civil court in which she was a defendant. At the same time, she basically drained all of her savings to pay attorneys to defend her in both the criminal and civil lawsuits against her. All that was really left were her interests in her business. One of her biggest concerns was that her boyfriend's mother also be protected.

We talked about a number of different possible solutions. From a planning perspective, Ava needed at the minimum a power of attorney and a healthcare directive in the event she became incapacitated. Based upon the financial assets she had left, including her interests in the business, I suggested she consider a few different options, including selling her share of the business back to her boyfriend's mother and using some of those funds to pay off the debts the business had incurred. I gave her a lot to think about.

At this point, I do not know what Ava decided to do. I know she was overwhelmed with all that was happening that was beyond her control. I am hopeful she will return to my office at some point so that I can help her get some form of an estate plan in place. But I recognize I can't always help everyone, even if I want to. Good luck, Ava—you still have some growing up to do, and I'll be here when you are ready.

Chapter 14

Fanciful Francine (Your Best Interests Are Not Automated)

Are you expecting the government to automatically process and distribute your assets to whomever applicable? Do you share property ownership with other people? And do you have any loved ones who live out of your country? Unfortunately, when left to automation, it's most likely that your assets will take the probate route—and I hope by this chapter you understand the dangers of this.

This next concept might be somewhat difficult for most of us to comprehend—but there is a slice of our society who believe that the government will "handle everything" after they die. A person who holds such a belief may feel a sense of assurance or reliance on the government's support. They may believe that the government will handle the distribution of their assets, provide for their dependents, or address any other relevant matters post-death—such as burial, creditors, and taxes.

In addition to erroneously believing that the government is going to handle it all for them after death, there could be several additional reasons that such a person might not want to prepare an estate plan. For example, they may misunderstand or have a lack of knowledge about the government's role in an estate matter. They might assume that the government automatically handles everything but not realize that without proper planning, the distribution of assets may be subject to legal complexities, delays, and potential disputes. They also may not realize that they would lose control of what happens to their assets should they pass away, believing falsely that the government will handle things on their behalf.

Some individuals may be uncomfortable with the idea of explicitly deciding how their assets should be distributed or managed after their death. They perhaps prefer to let the "chips fall" where they may. They may simply believe that their loved ones will sort things out on their behalf, or they are willing to leave these decisions to the government. There could be an element of procrastination here as well. Preparing an estate plan requires some time, effort, and expense, and requires potentially engaging with lawyers with whom they may not have had positive interactions.

Some people will postpone the task of creating their estate plan feeling that there's a lack of immediacy or urgency, a perception that it can just be done later. And finally, the person who believes they can rely upon the government may just be attempting to avoid the thought of their own mortality. Thinking about estate planning forces individuals to confront their mortality to some degree because they're planning for what happens after death. This can be emotionally challenging or uncomfortable for many people, and that discomfort may therefore lead them to delay or avoid undertaking the process altogether.

Of course, it is important to note that relying solely on the government to handle your estate matters can have plenty of unintended consequences. By not preparing an estate plan, individuals may lose the opportunity to express their preferences, protect their assets, minimize taxes, and provide for their loved ones in the most effective way. But again, that's not what is in the mind of the person who relies on the government.

With all that said, let's talk a little bit about Fanciful Francine.

Decades Unattended

When Francine came into my office for her estate plan, she was already 82 years old! She had outlived her husband and the majority of other family members, including her only child. While she had obtained her naturalized citizenship, Francine was from Denmark. This might explain why she believes the government would handle things for her. I'm not licensed in any other country—but I know that Denmark has free public health care and free public higher education including undergraduate and postgraduate universities. Moreover, they also have a government pension for retirement upon reaching a certain age. Given this context, it makes some sense that Francine believed that she did not even need an estate plan to pass her property and financial assets to her family members.

During the course of her marriage, Francine and her husband bought a single-family residence in the 1970s. In the early 1980s, they also purchased a vacation cabin up in the mountains outside of Los Angeles with Francine's unmarried uncle. The cabin itself was adjacent to a strip of land, which they also bought. Francine and her husband's shares were held in joint tenancy, and the two of them were tenants in common with her uncle.

Let me take a sidestep to explain some of these legal terms. There are multiple ways to hold title to property depending upon which state you live in. Joint tenancy is one such method. In a joint tenancy, two or more people co-own real property together. Each of the joint tenants has equal rights and equal responsibilities with regard to the property, and ownership is passed to the other joint tenant(s) upon the death of one joint tenant in equal proportions. The deed showing title will be recorded with the county recorder's office reflecting the joint tenancy ownership. Most often, joint tenants are related, such as husband and wife, parent and child, or siblings co-owning a property.

Another method of ownership is tenants in common. This is another form of co-ownership, but it's very different in that the property is not necessarily shared equally. Ownership can be equal or unequally divided between two or more people. More significantly, at the death of one tenant in common, their ownership rights do not pass to the other tenants in common but rather to the deceased owner's heirs (through probate if no estate plan is in place). Further, a tenant in common can sell their own interest in the property without affecting the ownership interests of the other tenants in common.

Francine and her husband paid off the cabin and the strip of land, and they covered the property taxes and insurance year after year. There was virtually no participation by the uncle other than his one-third share of the original down payment and his name remaining on the title.

In 1999, Francine's uncle passed away. He had no assets in his estate other than his interest in the cabin, and a whole bunch of debt. He never married and had no children. Francine and about 12 of her cousins (most of whom resided in Denmark) were the living heirs of the uncle. However, Francine and her husband did nothing about the uncle's name being on the title of the cabin. They just continued to live their lives, use the cabin, and pay what they had to pay.

First of all, from 1999 to 2022 is a heck of a long time to not take action! But what should have happened in 1999 when Francine's uncle died? Francine and her husband should have opened a probate to determine who was the rightful heir to her uncle's share of the property. Well, what they really should have done was encourage her uncle to create a Revocable Living Trust, despite not having much in assets, so that his family (Francine and her Danish cousins) could stay out of court! But, of course, neither of those things happened.

So here we are, 23 years later, and what might have been a relatively simple probate has turned into a complicated mess. Remember, following death, real property interests can only be passed either by a probated Will, an intestate succession probate (meaning there is no estate plan created by the decedent), a joint tenancy interest, or a Revocable Living Trust.

To compound the issue, Francine's husband passed away in 2019. Any guess as to whether Francine opened a probate after her husband passed away? Here is a hint . . .

NO, she did not.

So now, there were two estates that were potentially in need of probate—but neither of them were ever even started. Francine can thank her dear friend (my client) for encouraging her to, at the very minimum, speak to a lawyer. Had she not spoken to me, she would have passed this mess down to her relatives living in Denmark.

Optimistic Nonsense

Keep in mind, back in Chapter 2, I told you that probate cases in California can take from 12 to 18 months to complete! Can you even imagine the time, energy, and cost burden that would have been placed on those extended family members? Traveling to the United States, staying here for an unforeseen period of time, trying to understand and navigate the legal system in a country and potentially in a language that is unfamiliar to them.

I realize it is a unique circumstance to have your entire family living in a country other than the United States, but that does not mean the situation is exponentially easier for a U.S. resident. It just takes away some portion of the expense of international traveling and language barriers. Most people, including those who live in the U.S., are unfamiliar with navigating the court process and will hire competent counsel to handle the probate for them. Thus, the anxiety and stress, as well as the associated cost of probate, remain the same whether you live in this country or not.

Back to Francine for a moment . . . fortunately, Francine and her husband held their respective shares of the vacation cabin as joint tenants. When a joint tenant dies, their interest in the property is terminated and the property continues to be held by the surviving joint tenant. Therefore, all of Francine's husband's interests in that cabin transferred to her—no probate needed for that property interest. However, the uncle's share did not. Although her uncle had been deceased for more than two decades, his estate still owned a one-third interest in the vacation cabin. This HAD to be resolved before Francine passed away, or it would fall on her Danish family to deal with.

Uncle Sam Is Not Your Trustee!

If Francine had not come to me to create her own Trust, do you honestly think the government would have unraveled this complex mess? Nope—even though that is what Francine indicated she believed to be the case!

Most likely, when no one came forward to claim all of the properties she owned in California, the properties would have wound up in the California Department of Unclaimed Property. Can you imagine? And the answer to the question running through your mind is yes, the state can take real property as well as financial assets! A family home, a vacation home, and a strip of land next to the vacation home being held in perpetuity by the government of California. Mind boggling.

So, what steps should Francine have taken, and how did we unravel this mess? As noted above, when her uncle passed away without an estate plan in place, Francine and her husband should have opened a small-estate probate matter. They did not. However, they did take one very important step that made a substantial difference in the current situation.

Within a few months of her uncle's passing away, Francine and her husband hired an appraiser to appraise the vacation property. Good job! This is vitally important to provide to the probate court (at any point that the probate would be opened) to give a sense of the value of the deceased person's estate and provide a financial value to the specific property appraised.

Had Francine failed to get the appraisal in concurrent proximity to the death, the cost and difficulty in performing an appraisal, some 23 years after the fact, would be much higher and more complicated, as I'm sure you can imagine. The costs of everything have gone up! The value of this property today is about 35 times what it was worth in 1999, but that fact is irrelevant to the probate today. What matters to the probate court is what the property was worth at the time the partial owner died, not its value today. This did make things so much easier, except . . . notice still had to go out to all of the family members—in Denmark!

The moral of the story is that the government of your state is not going to help you distribute your assets to your family if you pass away without creating an estate plan that includes a Revocable Living Trust. Moreover, doing nothing in hopes that things will eventually "work out" after you've died is just nonsensical. Do all of your loved ones the favor of proactively planning for your assets, so that your fanciful ideas of what "might" happen down the line are not left to chance!

Chapter 15

Vibrant Vivian (You Don't Need to Learn the Hard Way . . .)

Have you made any of your wishes known to friends or loved ones? Do you have family members you may not trust with those decisions? Would you like to incorporate trustworthy individuals into your plans? Accidents are sadly inevitable, and with the right names on the right lines, your care and representation can be concrete. A little effort today may surprise you in the future.

If you are a single person, whether you have children or not, this story is for you.

Let me just put this out there: in my office, we do not discriminate against anyone. As long as my potential clients feel that I am the right fit for them and I feel that the potential clients are the right fit for my office, I will help them with their estate planning. It doesn't matter whom they love, how they worship, or how they live.

With that said, my preferred clients are people (single or married) with minor children. This is because, while I may have the wisdom and experience of practicing law for over 30 years, my number one job is as MOM. As a result, I have a true connection to the concept of planning to take care of my child during my incapacity and at the time of my eventual death. But the truth is, everyone over the age of 18 needs to have some form of a plan in place.

I've laid that foundation to tell you a story about a friend of mine, who happened to be a young, healthy, single woman. Meet Vivian.

Vivian lived in Arizona. She moved there from Tennessee when she was in her early 20s—in part, to get as far away as she could from her overbearing family. Vivian chose to start her life over in a place where she knew absolutely no one rather than remain in the small, isolated town she grew up in with a family that seemingly lived in the dark ages. Perhaps some of you can relate?

Her hometown was one of those places where everyone knew everyone, and being different meant you were judged—or even ostracized. Vivian never truly felt that she belonged in that town, or for that matter, with her biological family. She always had a very rocky relationship with her parents.

You see, Vivian was a very progressive, forward-thinking woman. She studied the benefits of exercise, yoga, homeopathic supplements, and holistic care. She truly believed in healing from a different perspective than anyone in the town where her family lived and worked.

Growing up, Vivian tried to live her life as the free spirit that she was. When it came to the old-school ideas of her parents, she rebelled. Mom and Dad did not understand Vivian's desire to teach others about meditation, spiritual healing, and the benefits of Eastern and homeopathic medicine. She did not initially tell any of her family members where she was moving. She basically up and left one day.

In Arizona, Vivian came upon a group of people who totally "got her" and the natural, healthy, spiritual way of life that Vivian knew she was destined to live. She found work doing weekly meditations, spiritual coaching, and administrative work with a large group of lawyers. While Vivian spoke very little about her family "back home," some of her friends knew she was estranged from her mother and other family members in Tennessee.

In addition, she confided in a few friends that her mother was actually an attorney. While Vivian had never aspired to be an attorney, she did feel pretty comfortable around them—knowing that she could offer her meditation and spiritual work to help those high-strung, stressed-out attorneys find a calm place. Now, I can tell you that I know A LOT of attorneys—and I think it's safe to say we could all use a little more calm in our lives!

After several years, when she was settled into her new life, new job, and new group of friends, Vivian finally let her family know where she was living. She did not speak with them often but maintained a healthy distance without totally cutting them off.

Although she wasn't an attorney, Vivian knew firsthand through her job the importance of estate planning. She had many discussions with the other coaches and attorneys whom she worked with about putting a plan together, and yet she didn't put a plan together.

She believed that since she was young, single, healthy, and vibrant, she was not yet ready for a plan. She took no steps to get any documents resembling an estate plan in place. She hadn't made estate planning a priority because she didn't have much in the way of assets. Ultimately, she figured she had plenty of time to get to "all of that."

Fast-forward to December of 2017. Vivian took a vacation during the time the company she worked for closed down for a couple of weeks so that everyone could reset before the start of the new year. Vivian decided to visit Utah to go skiing and spend time with friends over the holiday.

An Unexpected Tragedy (and a Series of Avoidable Events)

In one terrible moment, as Vivian was driving on an icy road in Utah, her little rental car was broadsided by an 18-wheeler. In an instant, this energetic and dynamic young woman was left barely clinging to life. Vivian suffered a brain injury, rendering her unconscious and comatose. It was not a good situation, to say the least.

Vivian's friends, who were her chosen family, knew what she would have wanted for herself in the event she was to become incapacitated. The problem was, Vivian had never put these desires into a legal writing that named someone to carry out her wishes. Her lawyer friends knew that for her care and recovery she would prefer CBD supplements, healthy foods, and holistic care, as opposed to painkillers, processed foods, and conventional treatment. They also knew Vivian would want her good friends to make decisions for her and handle her finances while she was incapacitated.

Initially, this was how it started. But during her stay in the hospital, the administration was able to track down Vivian's "next of kin": her mother, the attorney. Vivian's mother immediately flew out to Utah. She thought she knew how best to care for Vivian. She wanted to take Vivian out of Utah and back to

Tennessee—despite the fact that Vivian never would have wanted the type of care her mother thought was best.

Vivian's mother didn't want Vivian's friends to have access to her, and definitely didn't want Vivian to have holistic care. Her mother filed a court action to take over Vivian's financial and health care decisions. Vivian's attorney friends went to court against Vivian's mother. They tried as hard as they could to fight to have Vivian cared for in a way that they knew Vivian would have wanted.

The court battle cost Vivian more than $10,000—all of the money she had in the bank—to fight her mother taking Vivian back to Tennessee. Vivian's friends fought the good fight, but at the end of the day, a judge awarded guardianship to Vivian's mom. That's often how it works.

When there is no legal writing to the contrary, judges most often look to the immediate family in appointing these types of fiduciary roles. And since Vivian hadn't put her wishes into legal documents, the judge decided Mom was the right choice to take care of Vivian. He was wrong.

Even though Vivian's friends fought to ensure Vivian was cared for the way she would have wanted, her mother ultimately persuaded the judge to award conservatorship over her daughter and won the right to establish the care plan that she wanted. Vivian was moved back to Tennessee, precisely the place she had escaped from years before.

Vivian's mother cared for Vivian in her own way. Vivian eventually came out of the coma but had a very long road to recovery. It took years for her to recover sufficiently to be able to get out from her mother's grasp.

Lesson Learned

If only Vivian had learned from working among her attorney friends and had gotten even a few essential documents put in place, things never would have been left up to a judge—a judge who did not know Vivian or her specific desires with regard to her health and how she wanted to be cared for, or that her mother was the last person she would have wanted to direct her recovery.

You may recall the important documents that I mentioned in the Introduction. In Vivian's case, there were essentially three vital documents that she needed for her desires to be followed in the event of incapacity:

1. A Healthcare Directive (naming an agent to make healthcare decisions while Vivian was unable to do so for herself)
2. A Power of Attorney for finances (naming a person to handle Vivian's finances, pay bills, and so on during the time she was unable, such as when she was unconscious and in a coma)
3. A HIPAA waiver (where Vivian would name certain people to be given access to medical records and information about her medical condition)

Had Vivian executed those documents—setting forth her desire for the friends she wanted to care for her, in the manner she wanted to recover and recuperate from her injuries—she never would have wound up in the care of her mother. With those documents in place, a judge would not even have been necessary!

You may have the idea in mind that you are too young, vibrant, and healthy to need an estate plan. The truth is that we never know what life is going to throw at us. Once you become legal age (which is age 18 in most states), the law considers you to be an adult. (I know, questionable for many teenagers!) It is at that moment that you become vulnerable to having a judge name someone to act as a conservator over your money and over your health care decisions should you become incapacitated, unconscious, or comatose—unless you put at least the three documents mentioned above in place.

The good news with this story is that Vivian did recover from her injuries. She eventually moved back to Arizona and was able to put her plan together (with the help of an attorney licensed in Arizona), naming her dearest friends as her healthcare agents and powers of attorney. She set forth her desires in legal documents such that if anything else should happen to her, she had protections in place.

It was an expensive and time-consuming lesson. But Vivian's mother will never again have the power over Vivian's health care and finances.

All's well that ends well.

Conclusion (Are You Ready . . . to Get Ready?)

You did it—you read through all of these chapters! Okay, I am making an assumption. Perhaps you only read a few chapters; regardless, I thank you for taking the time to read at least some of this!

When I go back and look at what I've written across these pages, it reminds me that there are so many different people and personalities in the world (and sometimes it feels like I've met with all of them)! Everyone has their own unique story. Some have happier endings than others. At the end of the day, we all have one common factor—each of us, every single one of us, is going to die at some point in time. We can make a deal with the devil, we can pray to the almighty, we can even fight off and overcome diseases. Regardless, the reality is that death awaits us all.

(Hindsight Is 20/20)

In considering the various individuals about whom I've written, I wonder if you can see why some 68 percent of adults in the United States have not put an estate plan in place. There is excuse after excuse.

Looking back at some of the lessons from the individuals I've written about, did you find yourself in any of them? Could you relate to more than one? Did you discover reasons and excuses that you may have allowed to interfere in your own efforts toward putting your estate plan in place? Let's take a quick look back at the wonderful characters and the lessons they teach about the importance of pushing through their excuses.

Supported Sheila/Avoidance Arnie—hard conversations. First things first, you may need to have some hard conversations. They might be with your spouse, perhaps with a sibling, or maybe even with your aging parents. I call them hard talks because for most people, it is not easy to discuss money, incapacity, and death. But these conversations are so very necessary. In addition to talking about money, you may also need to discuss how children from a prior marriage factor into a blended family's estate plan. If you are like Sheila, you and your spouse may have completely different ideas as to how assets should be split. So don't be like Arnie and avoid these discussions. Start talking early and those conversations will get easier.

Clueless Cody—he knew absolutely nothing about estate planning. I want you to be like Cody and get educated! Again, one of the reasons that I love clients like Clueless Cody is because he didn't know what he didn't know. Yet, he also understood that he needed to learn! One of my greatest joys in estate planning is getting to educate people and then seeing the looks on their faces when they really start to "get it"!

Procrastinator Paul—couldn't make a decision and then died before finishing the process. This situation was tragic, and I would hate for this to happen to you or anyone you know. It is my philosophy that SOME decision is better than NO decision. Unfortunately, if the documents are not signed, there is NO decision. Remember that for the most part, a Revocable Living Trust (and all the supporting documents) can be changed as long as you are alive and have mental capacity. The moral of this story is, do not be like Paul and wait to get these plans in place! Otherwise, the very thing you would not want to happen is the most likely outcome!

Meager Melanie—thought she didn't own enough in assets to warrant a plan. Now you may think you don't have enough in terms of assets to require an estate plan, à la Meager Melanie. Hopefully, after reading her chapter, you can now see that there is more to it than simply how much money you have in the bank. All of your assets are taken into consideration for probate, not just the bank accounts. The probate threshold is different in every state, so you'll need to check with your local jurisdiction to know what that figure is. But if you own property or if you have minor children, those are also qualifying criteria for needing an estate plan to avoid probate.

Apathetic Andy—didn't care what happened after he died. This is not a scenario I see often, but if you simply do not care what happens to your assets after you die, my follow-up question is: Do you care about your family and loved ones and what they may have to go through if you do nothing? Similarly, if you have an adult child who may not be capable of making wise decisions around money (in my office, we refer to this as a "lifestyle disability"), do you want to leave them in charge of your hard-earned assets? Truth be told, Andy did care; he just did not realize that there was something that could be done to manage his assets by someone other than his alcoholic son. People, you just gotta ask!

Isolated Irwin/Skeptical Sue—avoided it because they didn't understand how to choose people they could trust. The common denominator for Irwin and Sue is that they did not have the traditional family dynamic, with siblings or cousins or someone they felt they could trust to manage assets on their behalf. Irwin needed guidance (and in some ways, permission) to choose someone who had more knowledge about his deceased wife's business to handle the job of Successor Trustee. Sue was more accepting of a licensed professional fiduciary. Failing to plan for either of these people would have been disastrous. Irwin's assets may have wound up with his deceased wife's family or the state. Sue's child would have wound up in child protective services, or with a brother she had disassociated from. Thankfully, they got their plans done in accordance with their desires. My advice for those of you who relate to these stories—talk to an experienced estate planning lawyer who can help guide you through the options available. The choices may wind up being better than you think.

DIY David—don't get me started here. Yes, I feel a great deal of frustration for the DIYers out there because they are setting their families up for failure. As you may recall, David's so-called estate plan was never even signed. Fortunately, his wife, Delia, thinks like me and knows there are some things that you need to hire a professional to do. Estate planning is definitely on that list. Some people don't like lawyers and do not want to hire them if they feel they can handle the job on their own. But I promise that not all of us are just here to make used car salesmen look good! Rest assured that some of us do care about our clients and keeping their families out of court and out of conflict.

Unfunded Uma—never moved her assets into her Trust. So, this story is one I liken to DIY David because Uma had a Trust plan drawn up by a lawyer; she is also a lawyer, and yet, she never moved her assets (including her real property) into her Trust! One of the most important steps in completing your estate plan is ensuring that all of your assets are moved into that Trust so that they can pass in accordance with the planner's wishes. If not retitled into the Trust, those assets would wind up going through the court process—and the reason Uma had a Trust created was to stay out of court. This is where which lawyer you hire to prepare your plan actually makes a difference. Most people need guidance, and some even want the lawyer to handle the transfers for them (totally doable) for an additional fee. At the end of the day, an unfunded Trust is not worth the paper it is written on! You definitely do not want to be like Uma and assume things are completely taken care of once the documents are signed. And if you work with a "traditional" estate planning attorney, this could happen to you too!

Prepared Patty/Prodigal Pete—there is a solution when one of you has a spending problem. We should all hope to inherit millions of dollars from our family. But even if the amount you receive from parents/family/others does not add up to millions, no matter how prepared you might think you are, without a proper estate plan in place, how would you keep your spouse from blowing that money on frivolous (or even not so frivolous) expenditures after you pass away? And for someone like Pete, who had a complex history with money, is it possible to talk about the past with empathy and not judgment? Estate planning offers so many different options and solutions to issues that you as the reader might think are esoteric or unique to you, when, in fact, there are likely others who have a similar, if not the exact, circumstance! We have a plan for you!

Overconfident Omar—thought he had all the answers, but really, did he? Not my favorite in the group, because there was really nothing I could have said to Omar to convince him his plan had holes in it. In dealing with this type of personality, I lay out the facts, the options, and the potential consequences. You can lead a horse to water . . .

Superstitious Sally—talking about death doesn't mean you'll bring it about. For most, this concept is common sense. For example, just because you want to win the lottery and talk about winning the lottery does not mean you're gonna win the lottery. (If only it were that easy!) Similarly, talking about and planning for death is not magically going to cause death to happen before whatever plan the universe has for us. Overcoming cultural biases takes not only a patient practitioner but a willing client. Not everyone falls into that category. And that is okay, because I'm just one lawyer and I cannot help everyone out there. Sometimes families will learn the hard way. I can live with that, knowing I tried my best and I am not in control of everything.

Cheap Charlie—the alternative to an estate plan is way more expensive (especially in California), and you leave all decisions up to a judge. That old saying "You get what you pay for" can be particularly true in the area of estate planning. If you do this on the cheap, you could wind up with documents that will not work the way you need them to and the way you intended upon your death. Of course, this won't affect you—but it can put your family in court and conflict. Don't be like Charlie! Instead, invest in a skilled, experienced estate planning attorney to get the job done right!

Adolescent Ava/Complete Cherise—is it ever too early to get started? In my opinion, no, it is not! Some forms of estate planning can take place as early as when a "child" turns the age of majority (18 in most states). We do not know what the future holds for us (except death, at some point). Get it done!

Fanciful Francine—the government is NOT there for you and your stuff. I do not believe that the vast majority of you readers think that the United States or state government will step in and handle your estate in a manner you would want in the event you pass away without a plan. In fact, I've detailed how probate works in my state—it is not a preferred path. Enough said.

Vibrant Vivian—planning also includes incapacity planning. Life brings with it many unexpected tragedies, whether we are young and healthy or old and decrepit. Two of the goals of planning are as follows: one, being prepared so your family (or a court) does not have to step in when something happens to you, and two, carrying out your own decisions as to how and by whom you want to be taken care of at incapacity. Vivian never would have chosen her mother to be her guardian, but she failed to plan.

So many of these folks never had to deal with a protracted probate after the death of a family member or deal with the court system's method of naming guardians for purposes of being a decision maker for health care and finances. If they had done so, my guess is that they would forgo the excuses and recognize the importance of making their own decisions by putting an estate plan in place before some calamity occurred.

Not that I need to remind you at this point, but I will—I practice as an estate planning attorney because of my daughter. At first, it was to get out of the courtroom and be at home to love and raise her. But then I became consumed with worry that something might happen to my husband and me, and then what would happen to our daughter? Who would raise her? How would a judge ever know who we would choose (or who we would definitely NOT choose) to be her guardian? And, heaven forbid, she would get our money all at once when she turned 18! But that is exactly what would happen if we died without a proper estate plan in place. I knew I had to figure out a way to help parents (and others) avoid the pitfalls that await the unprepared.

As a parent, these were my concerns. You may have other fears or concerns for what happens when you pass away. Perhaps you have a special needs child who needs to be cared for after you pass, or maybe you have a sizable estate and no close family to give it to. Whatever the circumstances are, I want to do my utmost to help you. Schedule a Family Wealth Planning Session with me so you can get better educated about your own situation, including what would happen with no plan and how we can change that trajectory. Because, truly, this is my passion now.

While I am here and available to serve people in California, I am only licensed in this one state. If you are reading this in another state and want my help, please reach out to me via my website, debrakovenlaw.com. I have a network of hundreds of firms in almost all 50 states, and I am confident I can refer you to a qualified estate planning attorney in your location to guide you through the process. If you are still unsure, you can subscribe to my website and follow my weekly tips and posts on Facebook, Instagram, and LinkedIn. Search Debra Koven Law, and you'll find me! Eventually, this will all make much more sense to you, and you'll wonder, *Why did I ever put this off? Debra made this so much easier than I thought it was going to be!*

To the Cheap Charlies in the room, I want to quickly address the fact that undertaking this important responsibility will always involve money. Ideally, you can find a professional who lists out their pricing and gives and explains to you the options you might want to consider. Every planning situation is different. Personally, I am not a fan of one-size-fits-all pricing, and my clients are able to select plans according to their unique situation. Overall, I want you to think about the part where not having anything in place leaves your loved ones vulnerable to losing some, if not all, of your estate to the probate process—on top of having no control over what happens, the proceedings very likely will overwhelm them. Grieving you will be enough for anyone to deal with.

The beauty of it all is that, while you cannot predict when your end might come, you CAN prepare for it in a number of ways that will ease your mind. You can relieve some of the stress and ensure that your desires are made known and followed so that the people, animals, charities, or causes near and dear to your heart are actually taken care of in the way you want them to be once you are gone.

I want to sincerely and humbly thank you for investing your valuable time in reading this book. I hope you found it informative and maybe even a bit entertaining. Wishing you only the best as you move forward in your life's journey. I hope it is a long and fulfilling one. Now, stop with the excuses, go out there, and get your estate plan done!

About the Author

Author Debra L. Koven is an estate planning attorney whose practice focuses on helping families with minor children in Southern California. She incorporates legacy planning for both monetary and intangible assets, as well as Kids Protection Planning®. Debra is the proud mom of one amazing daughter who arrived later in her life.

Debra graduated from the University of California, Los Angeles (Bachelor's degree) and Western State College of Law (Juris Doctor). She was honored in Who's Who of Professional Women and has belonged to numerous legal associations, including the State Bar of California, the Los Angeles County Bar Association, and Consumer Attorneys of Los Angeles. She is a certified Personal Family Lawyer®. From 1992 to 2010, Debra litigated hundreds of cases for injured people. Then, after her daughter was born, she switched to exclusively handling estate planning matters.

Debra's most important role is membership in the club of working moms who are balancing caring for a family and household and work, while not losing sight of their passions and personal goals. Debra is also an avid sports fan who loves to watch hockey, baseball, and college football—GO BRUINS!

She enjoys living near the beautiful beaches of Redondo Beach, California, with her daughter, Nyssa, her husband, Brad, and her cats Sammy, Ozzy, and Lily.

Made in United States
North Haven, CT
04 November 2026

21765027R00088